Basic Computers
For Beginne

By Web Wise Seniors, Inc.
An education program for beginning compu

Web Wise S
305 Wood
Eastlake, C
www.WebWiseSeniors.com

GAYLORD

PRINTED IN U.S.A.

I

Copyright

Trademarks

Limits of Liability/Disclaimer or Warranty

Sales Inquiries

For sales inquiries and special prices for bulk quantities, please call toll free (866) 232-7032.

Introduction

"The best computer class I have ever taken!" and "I never knew that computers could be explained so well!" are frequent comments made by Web Wise Senior students. Since 2000, Web Wise Seniors has successfully taught thousands of beginning computer users. Now, for the first time, the same teaching methods successful in Web Wise Seniors courses are found in this easy to understand book.

This book is not a reference for computers. It is a learning guide for people of any age who are unfamiliar with computers, but especially designed for seniors who want to be skilled computer users. It is like having a private instructor by your side as you walk through the basics of computer use with your book. This book is full of common questions, asked in real classes by beginners, with easy to follow answers that have already helped thousands.

Reading explanations and definitions will only get you so far. You need to actually use the computer to learn to use it, and this book will help you do just that. It will help you get started using the computer by walking you through basic skills step-by-step while answering your "whys" and "whats" along the way.

Web Wise Seniors teaches basic computer classes every day. WWS has seen what works, what doesn't work, and what beginners want to know first hand.

About the Authors

Web Wise Seniors is a company dedicated to teaching basic computer skills to individuals over the age of 50. Since 2000, Web Wise Seniors has filled over 22,000 classroom seats throughout Ohio, and has quickly become a premier computer education company for mature adults in the Midwest.

Classes have been designed for seniors by seniors and continually updated with the feedback of its students. By becoming an interactive part of the senior community and working closely with senior organizations throughout Ohio, Web Wise Seniors has been able to develop a unique teaching style and curriculum that has met with overwhelming success.

Since 2000, over 99% of Web Wise Seniors students said they would recommend the program to their friends and family. 100% of affiliated teaching locations have been happy to work with the WWS program and out of a 4 point scale, WWS received on average a 3.77 rating in student satisfaction.*

The same dedication and love of teaching that has made the WWS program so successful in the classroom is available for you in the pages of this book. Readers will find this book full of examples, illustrations, and easy to follow directions. This is a teaching guide, not just a manual or reference book.

*Student satisfaction as collected through WWS classes and events (2000 – 2006).

About this Book

Basic Computers for Beginners is designed to be read in order. Readers should begin with page one and continue through the book as if they were actually taking a computer course. The sections all relate and build upon each other.

Readers should keep a computer close at hand while reading *Basic Computers for Beginners*. We recommend you read through an entire section and then go back and try the steps outlined in the section.

Keep a pen or pencil handy too. Take notes and highlight any sections that you feel are personally important. This is your computer book and the more personal references you make within its pages, the better this course will work for you.

Above all, please enjoy Basic Computers for Beginners. Read at your own pace and keep at it. You'll be a computer wiz before you know it!

Make sure you
check out

Computer & Internet
Terminology
From

Included in the back of this book!

**Including a FREE BONUS section
on commonly used acronyms for
chat rooms and instant messenger programs.**

Meet Larry

Larry is the Web Wise Seniors mascot. He will be found throughout the pages of this book, helping you to "get the bugs out". Larry has been helping beginning computer users for over two years now. He answers commonly asked questions in the Web Wise Seniors' newsletter, runs the WWS help desk on <u>www.WebWiseSeniors.com</u> and often makes guest appearances in WWS publications.

In his spare time, Larry enjoys searching the Internet, e-mailing friends, and belly dancing.

Acknowledgements

We would like to thank the thousands of students that have challenged our computer instructors' minds in class. Your countless, and sometimes off-the-wall, questions and constructive feedback have made us better teachers. Without you, this book would not have been possible. Thank you!

We would also like to thank our family members for their insight, feedback, and support.

Credits

Authors
Michael Douglas
Stephen Pelton

Book Design and Production
Michael Douglas
Stephen Pelton

Proof Reading
Mary Pelton
Jean Pelton
Josette Bodonyi

Clip Art
Microsoft 2003 Clip Art Gallery

Screen Shots
Microsoft Windows XP

Table of Contents

Table of Contents

Chapter 3: The ABC's of Windows

Table of Contents

Chapter 4: Basic Skills

Table of Contents

Chapter 5: The Keyboard

Table of Contents

Chapter 6: Successfully Navigating through the Computer

Table of Contents

Chapter 7: Saving Your Work

Table of Contents

Chapter 8: Organizing Your Computer

Chapter 9: The Recycle Bin and More

Table of Contents

Chapter 10: Customizing Your Computer

Table of Contents

Chapter 11: Installing New Software

Table of Contents

Chapter 1

Basic Parts of a Computer

What You Will Learn in This Chapter
- ✓ The difference between desktop and laptop computers.
- ✓ Telling the difference between different computer monitors.
- ✓ An introduction to the keyboard, printer and mouse.
- ✓ The definition of an operating system.
- ✓ What your computer's processor does.
- ✓ What floppy disks & CDs are used for.
- ✓ How to safely handle floppy disks & CDs.

Chapter 1: Basic Parts of a Computer

Section 1: The Pieces and Parts

Desktop Computer

- A personal computer that is designed to fit conveniently on top of a typical office desk.
- A desktop computer typically comes with the tower, monitor, keyboard, and mouse. The modem, disk drive, and CD-Rom are located in the tower.
- Desktop computers are not portable but generally cost less than similar equipped laptop computers.

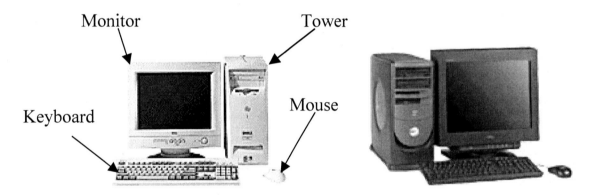

Monitor   Tower

Keyboard   Mouse

Laptop Computer

- A personal computer generally smaller than a briefcase that can easily be transported. Laptops have the ability to run on battery power.
- Laptop computers generally cost more than desktop computers with the same capabilities because they are more difficult to design and manufacture.

Chapter 1: Basic Parts of a Computer

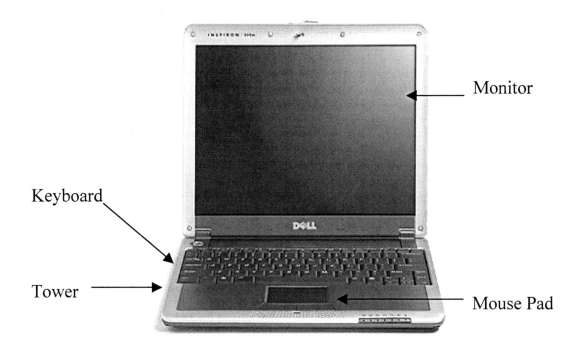

Monitor

Keyboard

Tower

Mouse Pad

Monitor

- A monitor resembles a TV. It contains the computer screen, which displays a picture of what you are working on. For example: If you are playing a game on your computer or typing a letter, you will see the game or the letter displayed on your monitor screen. Dot Pitch, Monitor Size, and Optimal Resolution are three terms often used when describing monitors.

1. <u>Dot Pitch</u>
- The image on your screen is made up of thousands of colored dots.
- The distance between a dot and the closest dot of the same color (red, green or blue) on a color monitor, measured in millimeters (mm).
- A smaller dot pitch means the dots are closer, which gives a sharper the image.

2. <u>Optimal Resolution</u>
- The recommended screen resolution for a monitor, measured in pixels (horizontal x vertical). Higher resolutions allow more information to fit on a screen.

3. <u>Monitor Size</u>
- Measured diagonally across the face of the monitor, from one corner of the casing to the other.

Traditional Monitor   **LCD Monitor**
                                 aka Flat Screen

Traditional Monitor Vs. LCD Monitor: What's the Difference?
- The traditional monitor has a much deeper back to it. It will take up more room on your computer table than the LCD monitor. An LCD monitor is commonly called a flat screen because its dimensions lack depth. An LCD monitor may be 3 – 5 inches thick while a traditional monitor may be 12 – 15 inches from front to back.

Keyboard
- A keyboard resembles a typewriter keypad. It is used to input information into the computer.

Chapter 1: Basic Parts of a Computer

Central Processing Unit (CPU)

- The brain of the computer. This part of the computer processes all the instructions from programs. The bigger the processor, the faster the computer.
- Processor speed is measured in megahertz (MHz).
- 1,000 megahertz equals 1 Gigahertz.
- Example, Intel Pentium III processor at 700 MHz is a slower processor than a 1 Gigahertz processor.

Printer

A printer is a separate piece of equipment that is connected to the computer. It takes an image found on the computer and transfers that image to a sheet of paper.

Printer

Computer Processor & Operating System

There are two basic parts of a computer that every computer needs in order to operate -- the computer's processor and its operating system. The processor of a computer for simplicity's sake is a "doohickey," a "gizmo," or a "thingamabob." Don't worry about the details, there are only two things you really need to know about the processor of a computer. First, the processor is found somewhere inside the computer and, unless you take apart your computer, you will never see it. The second important point is that the processor is the brain of the computer. It works like a traffic cop. The processor takes all of the commands that you give a computer and all of the information inside a computer and coordinates them to bring you results. In short, when the computer receives any type of information, that information is sent to the correct part of the computer through the processor. Without the processor you would have one big traffic jam of information.

Chapter 1: Basic Parts of a Computer

The operating system is the second important item that every computer needs. The operating system of a computer provides you with a way to interact with the computer. The operating system provides you with a way to input information into the computer. The menus, buttons, and pictures on your computer screen are what you refer to as the computer's operating system.

The operating system that most people are familiar with is called Windows. You may have heard of Windows 95, Windows 98, Windows 2000, Windows ME, or Windows XP. All of these operating systems are based on the same fundamentals. If you can use one of them, you can use all of them. All of these operating systems are upgrades of each other. Operating systems are upgraded in a similar fashion to cars. For example, the Toyota Camry has a new model every single year. Each year the Camry is updated and "improved," but that doesn't mean you have to go out and learn to drive a new Camry every year. You already know the basics of driving and those driving fundamentals stay the same. Only a few of the car's specific details change. The 2000 Camry may have new features or the automakers may change the location of certain items, such as the blinkers. Whenever I buy a new car, the first thing I look for is where the windshield wiper blades on/off switch is located. Every car seems to put the switch in a different place. I know where the switch is on my old car, and I know how to use it. But, even though I may not be familiar with the new model's switch location, I still know how to use it. The same ideas apply to computers and their operating systems. In this book you will explore Windows XP. But no matter what operating system you have, this book will help you.

The Mouse

Left Mouse Button   Right Mouse Button

"Tail" or Cord

Mouse: A hand held unit that allows you to control a white arrow displayed on the computer screen. This white arrow allows you to point to and select items on the computer screen. It is used to give commands to the computer. We will refer to this white arrow as the "mouse arrow" throughout this book.

Section 2: Places to Store Your Stuff

Hard Drive

The hard drive is the filing cabinet of your computer. Everything that is stored on your computer is stored in the computer's hard drive. Using a computer's hard drive to store information is very similar to using a traditional filing cabinet. The only major difference is that while you can physically touch a traditional file cabinet, you cannot actually touch the computer's hard drive or the information stored inside of it.

Both a filing cabinet and a hard drive have "drawers" and inside each of these drawers are "folders." Inside each of these folders, files or additional folders can be stored. A file refers to any item on your computer, such as a recipe, a letter that you've written, a photograph, etc. File cabinets and hard drives also share the same problem, the hardest thing about using either of them is remembering which folder you stored your favorite chocolate chip cookie recipe in!

Floppy Disk
- The floppy disk is a 3 ½ " x 3 ½ " flat plastic square device used to store information.

Chapter 1: Basic Parts of a Computer

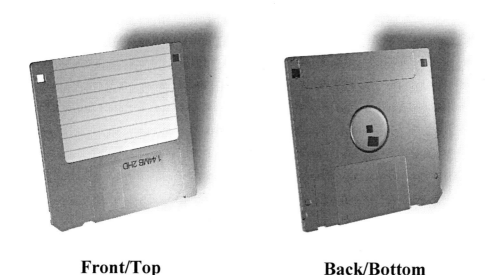

Front/Top   **Back/Bottom**

Computer users can store items such as letters, recipes, stories, and similar documents on floppy disks. The floppy disk is commonly used to store information because of its relative ease of use and its portability. After you save information to a floppy disk, you can take the floppy disk with you wherever you go. They are even small enough to fit in your pocket. The floppy disk is very similar to using a briefcase. You can store information in both a brief case and a floppy disk and take them with you wherever you go. When floppy disks are inserted into the floppy disk drive, the computer can gain access to the information stored on the disk.

Once information has been stored on a floppy disk, the information can be accessed, erased, or changed at any time. More than one item can be stored on a floppy disk. The computer will keep each item separate. Depending on how much storage room each item saved to a floppy disk takes up, a floppy disk can hold anywhere from one to hundreds of different items. When items are stored to a floppy disk, each item will be represented by its own icon (picture). To access the item you want to open, simply double click on the icon (picture). We will discuss accessing information on a floppy disk in more detail in Chapter 7: Saving Your Work.

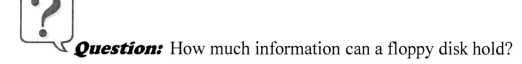

Question: How much information can a floppy disk hold?

Answer: A normal floppy disk can hold approximately 1,000 pages of black and white text. That's a lot of recipes!

Floppy Disk Drive

- The floppy disk drive is a 3 1/2" slot in the computer where you can insert a floppy disk.

On a *desktop* computer, the floppy disk drive is located in the front of the tower. On a *laptop* computer, the 3 1/2" slot is located somewhere along the base of the computer. Once a floppy disk is inserted into a computer, you can access the information already stored on the floppy disk and/or store new information on the floppy disk.

Inserting a Floppy Disk

You cannot insert a floppy disk incorrectly into a disk drive. It just won't fit. So, if you try to insert a floppy disk into the floppy disk drive and it won't slide in easily, you have the floppy disk either upside down, backwards or sideways. To insert a floppy disk correctly always look for the black or silver sliding door. See the floppy disk diagram on the next page. That sliding door goes in first. Next look for the metal silver circle. That silver circle is the bottom side of the floppy disk. Slide the floppy disk in until you hear a click.

Chapter 1: Basic Parts of a Computer

<u>Bottom Side</u>

Metal circle that faces the floor when inserting a floppy disk

Sliding door that is inserted first

Removing a Floppy Disk from a Computer

After you insert a floppy disk into your computer, a small button will pop out just above or below the 3 1/2" slot. Push that button into the computer and the floppy disk will pop out.

Warning: First, never open the sliding door on a floppy disk. Opening the sliding door exposes the sensitive material used to store data on a floppy disk. Opening the sliding door can ruin the stored information. Secondly, keep all floppy disks away from magnets. Magnets will erase everything stored on a floppy disk.

Compact Disk (CD)

- A compact disk, also known as a CD, is another portable storage device.

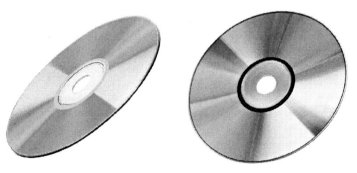

As with a floppy disk, think of a CD as a briefcase. You can store and transport information inside it. CDs are commonly used to store pictures, music, text documents such as letters and programs. In order to access or store information on a CD, you must first place the CD into a device called a CD ROM Drive. When inserting a CD into the computer, always put the CD in shiny side down.

Warning: When handling a CD, do NOT touch the shiny side of the disk. Hold the disk around the edges. Touching the shiny side of the CD may damage the CD and information may be lost.

CD ROM

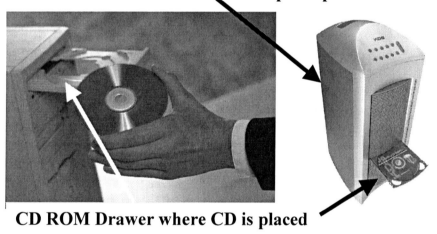

Tower on a desktop computer

CD ROM Drawer where CD is placed

A CD ROM is a device used to store or access information on a compact disk (CD). The CD ROM is a long rectangular drawer located on your computer. On a *desktop* computer, the CD ROM is usually located on the front of the tower. On *laptop* computers, the CD ROM is usually located on one of the sides of the laptop. The CD ROM will usually have a small button on the device located just below the drawer. When this small button is pushed, the CD ROM drawer will slide out of the computer. The CD may then be placed in this drawer and pushed back inside of the computer. Once the drawer has been closed, the computer will be ready to work with the CD.

Flash Drive

A Flash Drive is a third type of portable storage device becoming very popular in the computer world. What makes the flash drive so interesting is that it is a very small, easy to use, and durable device which can store a large amount of information. Flash drives allow information to be easily transferred from one computer to another or to be stored. Flash drives are small enough to be carried in a pocket or be attached to a keychain. In the picture to the right, you can see a flash drive has been placed next to a quarter to show you that, in comparison to floppy disks and CDS, flash drives are very small.

To use a flash drive, remove the cover protecting the flash drive's plug. Plug the drive into the USB port (socket) in your computer. Now, you can transfer information from the computer to the flash drive.

Flash drives are also called pen drives, thumb drives, key drives, USB Drives, and an assortment of other names.

Chapter 2

Let's Get Started!

What You Will Learn in This Chapter
- ✓ Tips to take the frustrations out of using a mouse.
- ✓ Turning the computer on & off safely.
- ✓ Right clicks vs. left clicks.
- ✓ When to double click & when to single click.

Chapter 2: Lets Get Started

Section 3: More About the Mouse

Don't Let the Mouse Discourage You

Learning to move and direct the mouse may be one of the most difficult skills you develop as you learn to use your computer. Listen to the hints on mouse use presented in this chapter, stick with it, and you will master the mouse before you know it. Most importantly, be patient with yourself.

Learning to Use the Mouse Correctly – YEAH!

Using the mouse can be one of the most frustrating things about learning to use a computer. Luckily, doing a few things properly can minimize this frustration.

First, you need to learn how to hold the mouse properly. People have the most trouble learning to use the computer when they hold the mouse like it has whiskers. Get a good grip on the mouse by placing your thumb on the inside of the mouse and your ring finger on the outside of the mouse. The front of the mouse should rest snuggly into the palm of your hand.

The tail of the mouse should ALWAYS point away from you. If you are holding the mouse correctly, the "tail" or cord of the mouse will go away from you. By holding the mouse properly, it forces you to keep the mouse-tail away from yourself. By pushing the mouse towards its tail, you will also be pushing the mouse away from yourself, which moves the mouse arrow up the computer screen. Pushing the mouse away from its tail, towards yourself, moves the mouse arrow down the screen. Pushing the mouse to its right moves the arrow to the right and pushing the mouse left will move the arrow to the left.

Holding the Mouse Correctly: Visual Guide

Top View:
Thumb on
inside & ring
finger on the
outside.

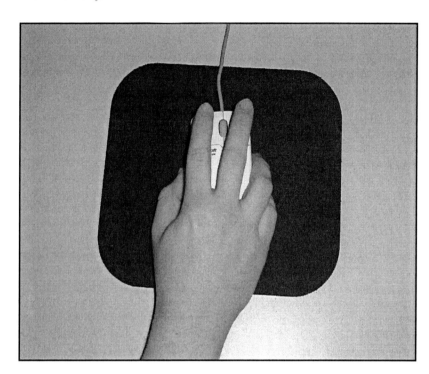

Outside View:
Index &
middle finger
do NOT rest on
top of mouse.
Index &
middle finger
are kept raised
in the air.

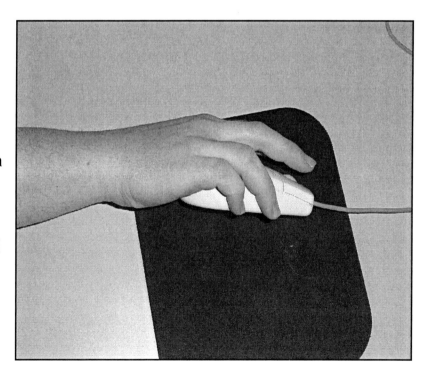

Chapter 2: Lets Get Started

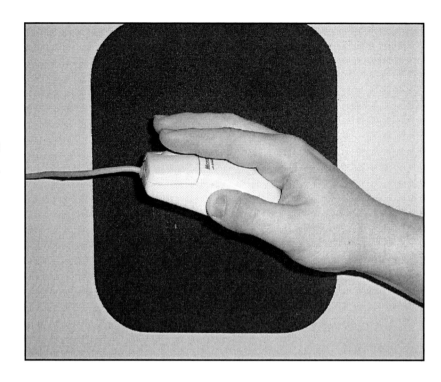

Inside View: Keep a good grip on the mouse.

The mouse must be moved on a smooth flat surface to work. Pick the mouse up and move it around in the air, you will see that the mouse arrow on the computer screen will not move. It is important to note this aspect of the mouse because it provides you with the solution to one of the most common problems associated with mouse use.

Often times, a new mouse user runs out of space on the desk when using the mouse, reaching too far to the left or right trying to guide the mouse arrows across the computer screen. Occasionally a new student will run the mouse off the table or into the computer while attempting to move the mouse arrow to its destination. You can avoid this pitfall by simply picking the mouse up and placing it down on the table where you have more room to roam. Remember, while the mouse is in the air, the mouse arrow on the screen will not move. The mouse arrow stays still until you place the mouse back down and begin rolling it on a smooth surface again.

The Mouse and its Buttons

The mouse typically has two buttons. These buttons are referred to as the left and right mouse buttons. The left button is used to select an object on the screen or perform an action. When you want to tell the computer to do something, you simply place the mouse arrow over an object and *gently* press the left mouse button one time. This is called a <u>single click</u> or a <u>left click</u>.

Sometimes you have to perform an action called a <u>double click</u>. A double click is two quick clicks, *gentle* presses, of the left mouse button. Double clicks are usually used to open/activate icons. Icons will be explained further in Chapter 3: Section 6. When performing a double click, it is important to keep the mouse completely still. If the mouse moves at all during a double click, the double click will not register. To avoid moving the mouse during a double click, try to click the mouse lightly. Hard clicking will cause the mouse to move.

 ***Hint:*** Don't click too much. Remember, each time you click the left mouse button you are telling the computer to do something, so be very careful with your clicks.

The Right Mouse Button

While you are first learning, you can do everything you need to do with the left mouse button. The right button is used to bring up a shortcut menu. Advanced users use the right mouse button to perform actions listed in this menu. Throughout this book, you will never need to use the right mouse button.

It is important to understand what happens if you accidentally press the right mouse button. If you accidentally press the right mouse button, a gray menu (looks like a gray box) will appear on your computer screen. To get rid of the gray menu, simply move the mouse arrow so it is NOT touching the gray box and press the left mouse button one time. The gray box will disappear.

Section 4: Turning the Computer ON and OFF

How Do I Turn the Computer ON?

All computers have power buttons which are used to turn the computer on. The location of a computer's power button changes depending on the type of computer you have, but all power buttons have the same symbol on them. The power button looks like a circle with a line at the top. If you have a desktop computer, the power button will be located on the tower (the big square box). Older computers may require you to turn on your monitor separate from the computer, but the monitor's power button will have the same symbol on it. Laptop computers and newer computers have one power button that turns on the computer and its monitor at the same time. A laptop power button is typically located above the keyboard near the monitor.

To turn your computer ON, press the power button one time. Do not hit the power button multiple times. It may take the computer a couple of minutes to turn on. If the computer goes to the desktop, you are ready to begin working with your computer. The desktop screen is illustrated below.

This is your desktop.

If your computer takes you to a log in screen, illustrated below, you will have to "log in". Logging in is a simple process. Place the mouse arrow above your user name on the log in screen and click the left mouse button one time. A successful left click will send you to your desktop where you can begin working.

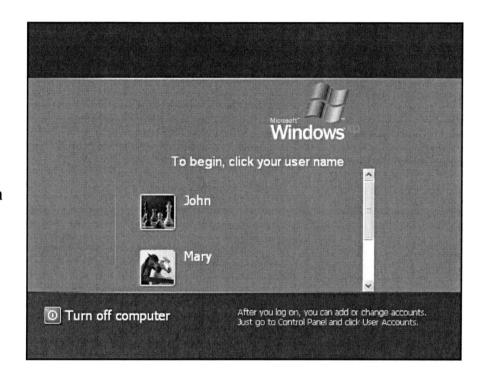

This is an example login screen.

 QUESTION: What is a log in screen?

ANSWER: Some computers use log in screens so several people can use the same computer while keeping their information separate. For example, Mary and John share a computer. Mary wants to keep the work that she does on the computer separate from the work that John does on the computer. In order to do this, two separate accounts can be created on the computer, one account for Mary and one for John. After the two accounts have been created, whenever the computer is turned on, the computer will automatically go to a log in screen where John can choose his user account or Mary can choose hers. Any information that Mary or John save to the computer will only appear in their account. Any changes that Mary or John make in the computer will only affect their individual account. Having more than one account on a computer allows people to share a computer while keeping their work private and separate from other accounts.

If you are the only person using your computer and only one account has been created, you will NOT go to a log in screen when you turn your computer on. You will go directly to your desktop screen.

QUESTION: What is a user name?

Answer: Computers use USER NAMES to identify who is using the computer at the time. If more than one person uses the same computer, user names are used to instruct the computer to keep everyone's work separate and private. The user name will appear on the log in screen explained above. In the previous example, Mary and John both used the same computer. When they turn on their computer, they will go to the log in screen. The log in screen will contain their user names. John's user name is JOHN and Mary's user name is MARY. To begin working, they will have to select their user name by clicking on it once with the left mouse button.

Example log-in screen showing two different users.

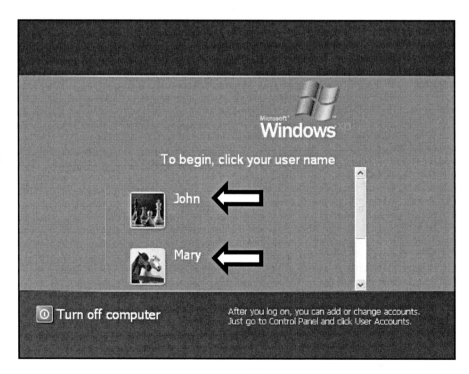

Chapter 2: Lets Get Started

After you log-in you will go to your desktop.

How Do I Turn the Computer OFF?

WARNING: Do not turn your computer off by pulling the plug or pressing the power button. If you do, you may corrupt (destroy or damage) the files you have on your computer. The proper way to turn your computer off is to first close all of the programs open on your computer screen. This means that you should not have any windows open on your desktop or on the task bar. Windows will be explained in detail in Chapter 3. You can close your programs by clicking the "X" in the upper right hand corner of any window. After you have closed all programs and are staring at a clean desktop, click on the "Start" Button to open the Start Menu. Highlight TURN OFF COMPUTER by placing your mouse arrow above it and then select TURN OFF COMPUTER by clicking your left mouse button once.

A window will appear in the middle of your computer screen with three options. The three options are Hibernate, Turn Off, and Restart. Place your mouse arrow above the option TURN OFF and click the left mouse button one time. When you select TURN OFF, one of two things will happen. Either your computer will turn off OR your computer will go to a screen that tells you "It is now safe to turn off your computer." If your computer screen goes black, it has turned off and you are done. If your computer goes to a screen that tells you "It is now safe to turn off your computer," you will need to press the power button on the computer one time. Your computer will turn off.

Following these steps will enable you to turn off your computer properly and safely whether you are working with a laptop computer or a desktop computer. However, if you have an older desktop computer, you may need to turn off your monitor as well. It is safe to turn off your monitor by pressing the power button located on the monitor.

Turning Off the Computer: Step by Step Instructions
1) Close all programs.
2) Click on START
3) Click on TURN OFF COMPUTER
4) Click on TURN OFF
   - Some computers will turn themselves off without you having to press the power button. This is most likely for laptops and newer desktop computers.
   - If you have a desktop computer and the monitor does not turn off automatically, press the power button on the monitor.
   - If your computer goes to a screen that states "It is now safe to turn off your computer" press the power button.

QUESTION: How often should I turn my computer off? Is it safe to leave my computer on all the time?

ANSWER: Some people leave their computers on all of the time. Other people turn their computer off after every use. Neither of these habits will necessarily damage your computer. From personal experience, I have found that avoiding extremes with computers is usually a safe rule to follow. Don't leave your computer on all the time, don't turn it on and off ten times a day, and avoid letting it sit around unused for weeks on end. If you are going to use your computer periodically throughout the day turn it on in the morning, leave it on all day and then turn it off before you go to bed. If you only use your computer once a day, turn it off after use. Simply stated, avoid extremes.

WARNING: If you have high speed Internet access, such as DSL, it's best to shut off your computer when you are not using it. Leaving your computer on while connected to high-speed Internet access lines leaves your computer more vulnerable to viruses.

Turning Off the Computer: Visual Guide

Step One:
Click on the
START button

**Step Two:
Click on the
option
TURN OFF
COMPUTER**

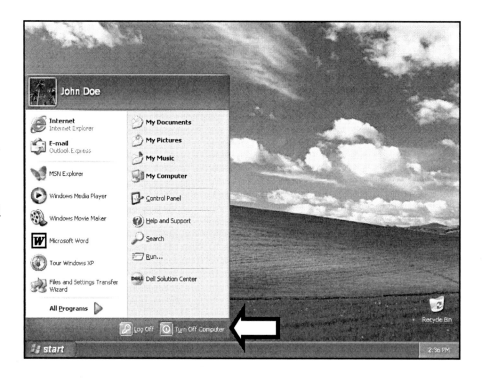

**Step Three:
Click the
TURN OFF
button**

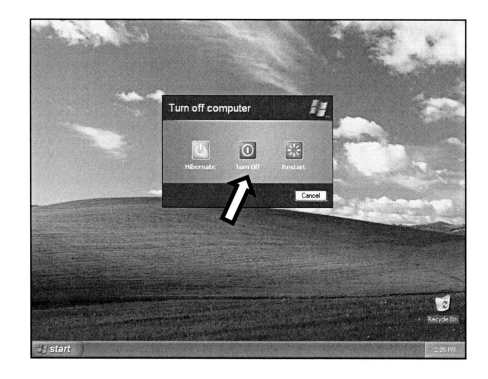

Chapter 2: Lets Get Started

Section 5: Mouse Clicks & Tricks

Making the Mouse Easier to Use

There is a great exercise that you can do to help improve your mouse skills. While holding the mouse, rest your wrist on the desk. Without removing your wrist from the table, try to move the mouse arrow from one side of the computer screen to the other. This is very difficult to do unless you have an extremely flexible wrist. To perform this task correctly, roll the mouse one inch in one direction, pick the mouse up and return it to its starting position. This entire process is performed without removing your wrist from a stationary position. Repeat this process until the mouse arrow has gone from one side of the screen to the other. If you are doing this exercise correctly, your mouse movement should resemble that of petting a dog...move the mouse left, pick it up and return it its starting position, move the mouse left, pick it up and return it to its starting position. This is the proper way to move the mouse arrow around the computer screen.

If you use the mouse correctly, you will never move the mouse more than an inch in any direction enabling you to use the mouse in a very small area. This simple exercise will teach you how to use your mouse over a smaller area.

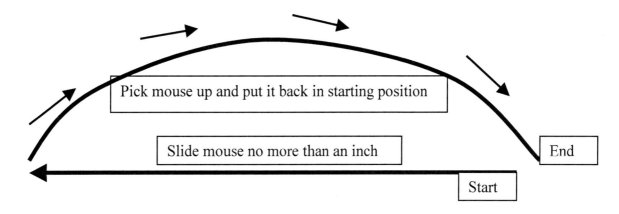

Chapter 2: Lets Get Started

The Single Click

A single click is pressing a mouse button down one time. Single clicks are used to highlight icons in blue, select options in menus, and press buttons on your computer screen.

The Double Click

A double click is quickly pressing down the left mouse button two times in a row. Double clicks are used in many situations but, most commonly, to open up or activate icons on the computer.

Question: When do I double click and when do I single click?

Answer: The most common question asked by students in classrooms is "when do I double click and when do I single click?"

There are two rules of thumb. The first rule is use double clicks whenever you recognize something as an icon. If it's not an icon, don't double click it. Icons are discussed in further detail in Chapter 3: Section 6. The second rule is if you are not sure whether or not an item is an icon, then single click it. If nothing happens, then double click it.

Warning: Never dive in with a double click. If you double click something that is supposed to be single clicked, the extra click may move you past an important screen.

Double clicking can be tricky. It is very common to double click icons and have nothing happen. Do not be discouraged if this happens. If you double click an icon and nothing happens, one of several things may have gone wrong. Here are some hints that will help improve your double clicking.

Hint: The speed of your double click is important. If you double click too slowly the computer may not respond. Try clicking a little quicker.

Hint: Always click on the picture part of the icon. Do not click on the words below an icon.

Hint: Keep the mouse as still as possible when double clicking. If you move the mouse at all while double clicking, the double click will not register. People often move the mouse while double clicking because they press the mouse button down too hard. Be gentle and press the mouse buttons down softly.

If all else fails: If you cannot open up an icon with a double click, there is an alternative. Single click an icon and it will become highlighted, in other words, the icon will turn blue. After you turn the icon blue, press the ENTER key on your keyboard. Pressing the ENTER key on the keyboard while an icon is blue (highlighted) will bring about the same results as a successful double click.

Chapter 2: Lets Get Started

Chapter 3

The ABC's of Windows

What You Will Learn in This Chapter
- ✓ What items make up your computer's desktop screen.
- ✓ How to open up programs located in your Start Menu.
- ✓ What a "window" is.
- ✓ The basic characteristics of "windows".
- ✓ Working with more than one window at a time.

Section 6: Introducing Your Desktop

Introducing your Desktop

The Background

The desktop is the screen your computer uses as its starting point. The desktop is usually the first screen that appears after you turn your computer on. If you have to log into your computer, the desktop will be the first screen that appears after you log in. Most computer desktops share the same qualities and items. First, all desktops have a background of some type. The desktop shown below has a picture of green fields. The background of your desktop can be changed, so do not be alarmed if you are looking at your desktop and you have a different picture.

Your Desktop Screen

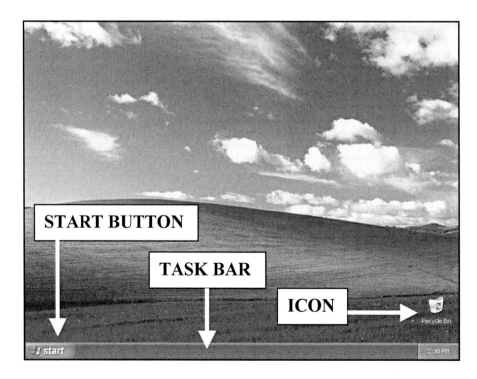

Icons

The second item that most desktops have is icons. Icons are little pictures that represent shortcuts to different places on your computer. Most icons represent shortcuts to items stored in your Start Menu. Icons are customizable, so once again, do not be alarmed if you only have one icon or twenty-five. To activate an icon, you have to place the mouse arrow on the picture and double click. In the example below you have one icon known as the Recycle Bin. Further on in this book we will discuss the procedure of placing your own icons on the desktop.

Task Bar (Status Bar)

The gray bar along the bottom of your desktop is known as your task bar or status bar. You will see further along in this book how important the task bar is in keeping track of the programs you will be using.

The Start Menu

The Start Menu is the fourth common item found on desktops and the most important. The Start Menu is located in the lower left hand corner of your computer screen. The Start Menu is important to learn how to use for two reasons. First, the Start Menu contains everything in your computer. If you ever need to find anything, you can always open your Start Menu and locate it. The second reason is that the Start Menu will be the first menu system that you work with on the computer. If you figure out how to use the Start Menu, you will be well on your way to understanding and using every menu system in the computer!

Section 7: Working with your Start Menu

More About the Start Menu

To open the Start Menu, place the mouse arrow on the START Button. Click your left mouse button one time and the Start Menu will open. Once the Start Menu has been opened, you navigate through the Menu by simply moving your mouse arrow up and down the options. You do not need to click your mouse as you move through the Start Menu.

Chapter 3: The ABC's of Windows

Take a look at the start menu. It is filled with different topics including "All Programs", "Shut Down", "Search", "Run", and many more. Each of these topics represents a different location or function of the computer. In order to choose any of these topics, place your mouse arrow on the option you want and click the left mouse button one time.

Hint: Single click when you choose your item in the Start Menu. Double clicks are NOT needed in the Start Menu.

Opening Solitaire

Let's run through opening a game of Solitaire on the computer. This is a great exercise because opening up Solitaire on the computer uses the same process as opening all of the other programs.

Without clicking, take your mouse arrow and move it around the Start menu. As you move your mouse arrow around the Start Menu, notice that whatever topic the mouse arrow is located on top of becomes highlighted in blue. Whenever an item is highlighted in blue, the computer is ready to work with that item. Knowing where your mouse arrow is located and what is highlighted is important because, if you press your left mouse button while an item in the menu is highlighted, you will activate that option. You need to be very selective with your mouse clicks. Do NOT click until you have found the Solitaire option.

Notice that some topics such as ALL PROGRAMS have arrows next to them that are pointing to the right. These arrows tell you that there is more information underneath that topic heading. In order to see the additional topics, take your mouse arrow and place it on the topic with the arrow. In this case, place your mouse arrow on top of ALL PROGRAMS. ALL PROGRAMS will become highlighted in blue and a submenu will appear displaying the programs on your computer. In order to move your mouse arrow into the submenu, you must slide your mouse arrow into the submenu without moving outside of your blue highlight. If you move the mouse arrow outside of the blue highlight, the submenu will disappear. If the submenu disappears, simply move your mouse arrow on ALL PROGRAMS and try again.

Once you have moved your mouse arrow into the submenu, you may then move your mouse arrow up and down within the submenu. Notice that in the ALL PROGRAMS submenu, some of the topics also have arrows next to them. This means there is yet more information underneath those topics. Slide your mouse arrow on top of the option GAMES, and a new submenu will appear containing all of the games on your computer. To slide into this next menu you must slide your mouse arrow directly across into the games menu without leaving the blue highlighted area. Once you are in the GAMES submenu, move your mouse arrow until it is directly on top of the option SOLITAIRE. SOLITAIRE will be highlighted when your arrow is on top of it. Once SOLITAIRE is highlighted, click the left mouse button one time to tell the computer that you would like to play a game of solitaire. If you click successfully on the option SOLITAIRE, a Solitaire game will open up on your computer screen.

If at any time you get lost or this process seems overwhelming, move your mouse arrow away from the Start Menu so that your mouse arrow is not touching any part of the Menu and click the left mouse button one time. By clicking away from the Start menu, you tell the computer you no longer want to work with the Start menu. The menu will disappear and you can start from scratch.

Question: How did you know where Solitaire was located?

Answer: The answer is practice. You need to be curious about your computer. Open up the Start Menu and practice navigating around through the menu. Click on different options and see what happens. You will learn very quickly where items are in the Start Menu.

The menu is set up very logically. Any time there is a black arrow next to an option, there is more information under that topic. These topics start off general and become more and more specific. The topic names are there to help you understand what may be stored within its submenu. When an option does not have a black arrow next to it, that means the option is an actual item. If you click on it, you will activate some screen or program on the computer. In the previous example of opening up Solitaire, the options you highlighted had black arrows next to them except Solitaire. Since Solitaire did not have a black arrow next to it, when you clicked on it, Solitaire opened.

Common Pitfall: Whenever you click your left mouse button to make a selection on the computer, it is very important to keep your mouse completely still. If you move your mouse at all, your click will not register. This is especially important when working with your Start Menu. If you move your mouse while clicking, you may accidentally remove programs from your Start Menu. Obviously you do not want to do this, so concentrate on keeping your mouse still. One major reason people tend to move their mouse while clicking is that they click too hard. Be gentle with your clicks.

Opening Solitaire: Step by Step Instructions
1. **Click on the START BUTTON**
2. **Highlight the option ALL PROGRAMS**
3. **Highlight the option GAMES**
4. **Highlight the option SOLITAIRE**
5. **Click on the option SOLITAIRE**

Opening Solitaire: Visual Guide

**Step One:
Click on the
START button.**

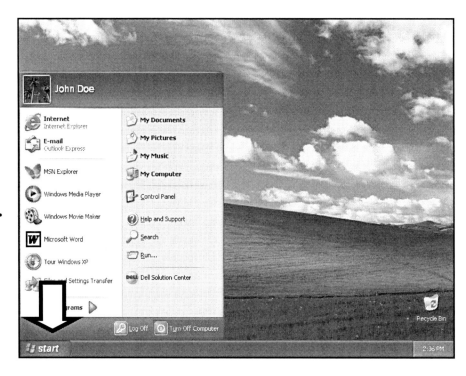

Step Two:
Highlight
ALL
PROGRAMS

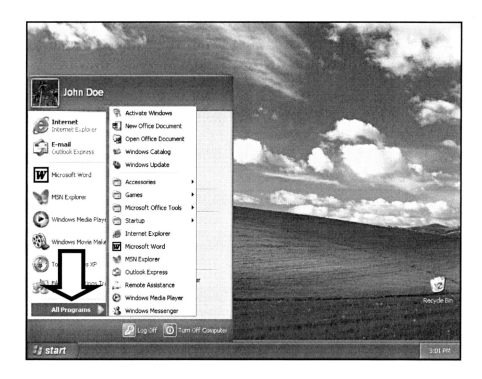

Step Three:
Slide into the
PROGRAMS
Menu &
Highlight
GAMES

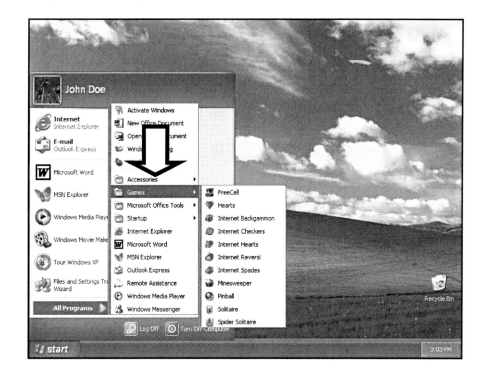

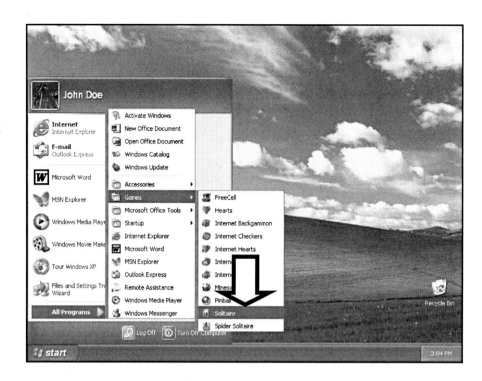

Step Four:
Slide into the
GAMES Menu
& highlight
SOLITAIRE.

Step Five:
Click on the
option
SOLITAIRE.

Step Six:
The game of
Solitaire will
open up in a
new window.

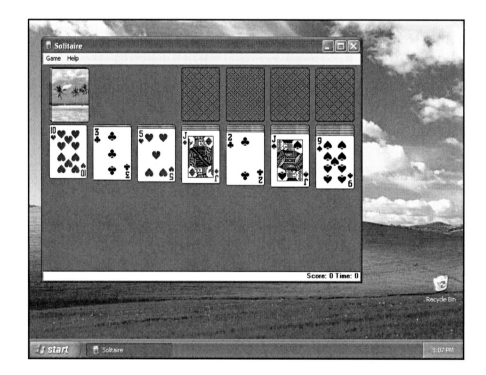

Section 8: Working with Windows

Window Characteristics

The game of Solitaire opens up in a window. Any program you work with on a computer will open in a window. This is important because nearly all windows have the same basic characteristics. If you understand the basic characteristics of a Solitaire window, you will understand the basic characteristics of almost every window you ever encounter. The four main window characteristics you need to be familiar with are: The Title Bar, the menu Bar, the Minimize, Maximize, and Close Buttons, and the corresponding buttons on the task bar.

Title Bar

The title bar is located at the top of every window. The title bar is important to check because it tells you where you are on the computer and what window you are currently working with. Notice that the title bar is telling you that this is a Solitaire window.

Title Bar

Menu Bar

The menu bar is located directly beneath the title bar. The menu bar contains options that will affect information in the window. Different windows will have different numbers of menu options as well as different topics. The Solitaire window you are working with has two menus: GAME and HELP.

Menu Bar

Corresponding Task Bar button

Whenever you open up a program on the computer, it will appear in two places. You will get a window on the desktop and a corresponding button on the task bar. This is true for every window that you work with. The title of each window, displayed on the window's title bar, will match the name on its corresponding button on the task bar.

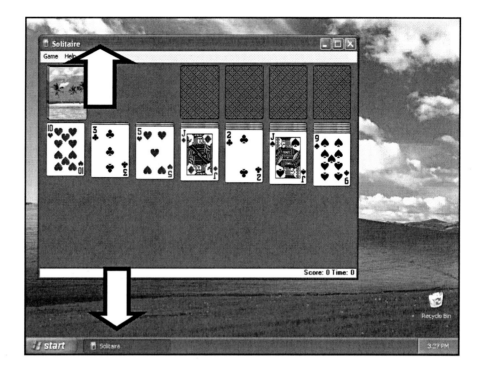

The button on the task bar matches the title bar

Minimize

The minimize button is located in the upper right hand corner of the window. The minimize button has a minus sign on it. Minimize removes the window from the screen, but does not close it. Your information is not lost. It is hiding. In fact, it is hiding under its name in the task bar. When you minimize a window, the window is stored on your task bar at the bottom of the screen. To retrieve your window, simply place your mouse arrow above the button on your task bar that represents the minimized window and press the left mouse button once. The window will return to the computer screen.

The minimize button comes in handy when you need to see what is behind a particular window. It is useful in clearing away windows from a "cluttered" desktop without completely closing a program.

The Minimize Button: Visual Guide

**Step One:
Click on the
minus sign.**

**Step Two:
Click on the
window's task
bar button to
bring the game
of Solitaire
back.**

**Step Three:
The window
has returned.**

Maximize/Restore

The maximize button has one big square on it. When you press the maximize button your window will stretch out to cover the entire computer screen. After a window has been maximized, the symbol on the maximize button changes. The one big square symbol turns into two small squares. This change occurs in order to tell you that you cannot make the window any larger. If you click the maximize button again the window will restore itself to its original, smaller, size.

The Maximize Button: Visual Guide

Step One:
Click on the middle button symbolized by the square.

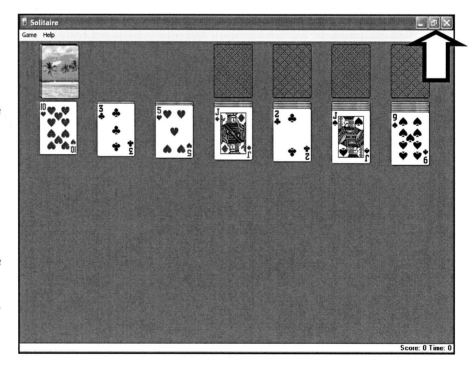

The window will stretch to cover the entire screen.

Step Two:
Click on the middle button again to restore the window to its original size.

**Step Three:
The window
has been
restored to its
original size.**

Close

The close button is located in the far right corner of each window. The close button has a big "X" on it. The close button will remove the window from the computer screen as well as remove the window's button from the task bar. Unsaved information will be lost.

The close button will be your worst enemy and your best friend. It will be your worst enemy, for example, if you are playing a game of solitaire and you are about to win. If you accidentally click on the close button your game of Solitaire will be lost. It will be lost forever. If you wanted to start a new game of Solitaire, you have to re-open the program by going though the Start Menu again. The close button will be your best friend because it will get rid of almost any window. This is important because, once you are familiar with the close button, you should never be afraid to experiment with your computer. Be curious and click on everything in your computer to see what it is. If you ever get lost or don't like what pops up, simply place your mouse arrow on top of the close button and give one click.

The Close Button: Visual Guide

Step One: Click on the "X" to close the window.

Step Two: The window has been closed. The window has been removed from the desktop and the task bar.

Chapter 3: The ABC's of Windows

Using Menus

The menu bar is located directly beneath the title bar. The menu bar contains options that will affect information in the window. Different windows will have different numbers of menu options as well as different topics. The Solitaire window you are working with has two menus: GAME and HELP. These menus work in a very similar fashion to the Start Menu. To open any menu on a menu bar, place your mouse arrow on top of the menu you want to open and press the left mouse button one time. The menu will open. Without clicking again, move your mouse arrow down the menu until the mouse arrow is on top of the option you want. If your mouse arrow is successfully placed on top of the correct option, the option will be highlighted in blue. Click your left mouse button one time and the option will be selected.

Try using the menu bar in the Solitaire window. You have two options: GAME and HELP. Click on the option GAME and a menu will appear containing five options. These options are DEAL, UNDO, DECK, OPTIONS and EXIT.

Move your mouse arrow down to the option DEAL. Once the option deal is highlighted in blue, click the left mouse button one time. If you successfully clicked on DEAL, a new hand of Solitaire will have been dealt.

Try another one. Click on the menu GAME again and move your mouse arrow down to the option DECK. Click your left mouse button one time on DECK, and a small rectangle should appear with several styles of card backs on it. This option enables you to change the design on the backs of the playing cards. In order to do this, place your mouse arrow over the card design of your liking, and press the left mouse button one time. The card back should now have a blue rectangle around it. The blue rectangle tells the computer that this is the card back you have chosen. Next, you then have to tell the computer it is OK to make the change, so click the OK button at the bottom of the window and the design of the back of your card deck will be changed.

Have fun with menus. Open them up and click on different options. See what happens. If anything strange happens or you get lost, simply click the close button in the upper right hand corner of the window. The Close button is explained on page 43. As you work with computers more often, you will begin seeing similar menus and options throughout different windows.

Using Menus: Visual Guide

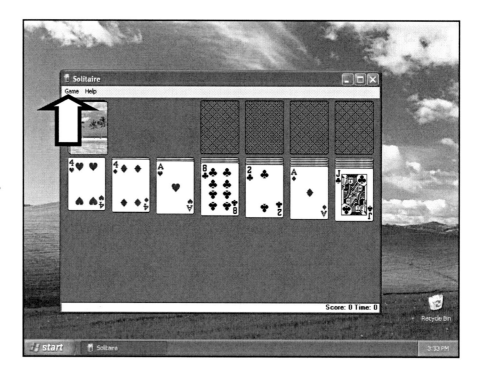

**Step One:
Click on the
menu GAME.**

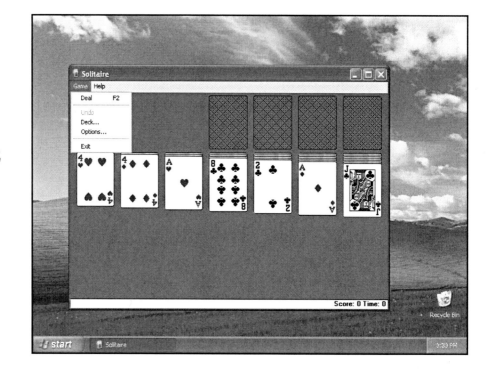

**Step Two:
The GAME
menu will
open.**

Step Three:
Slide the mouse
arrow down to
the option
DEAL and
click once.

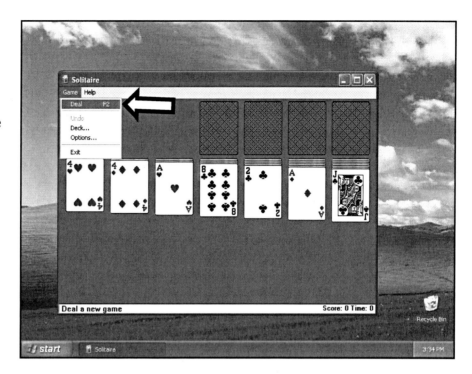

Step Four:
A new set of
cards has been
dealt.

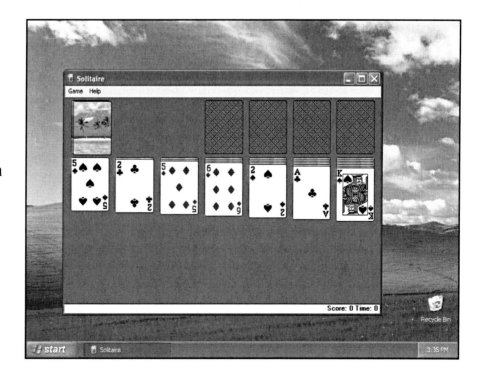

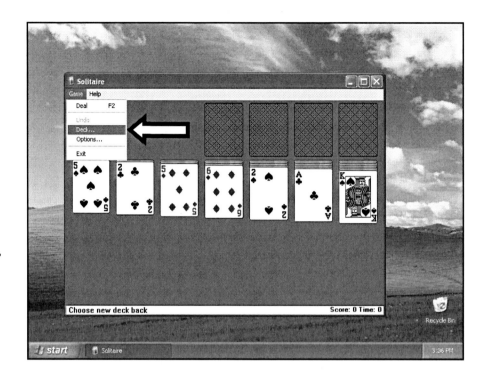

Try another
option:
Click on the
GAME menu
and select the
option DECK.

A small screen
will appear
that enables
you to change
the design on
the back of
your cards.

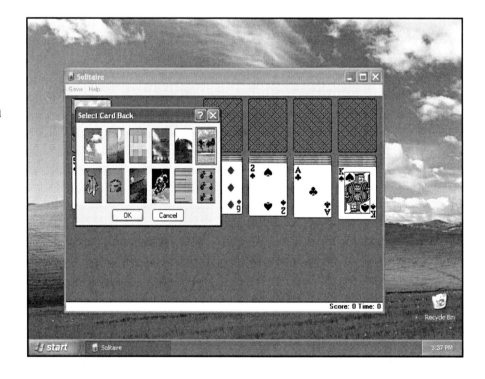

Click on the design you like. To select it and then click on the OK button.

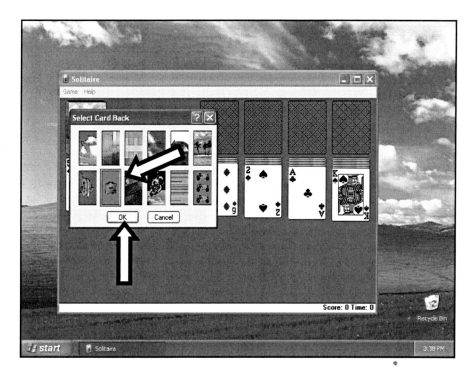

The design on the back of your cards has been changed.

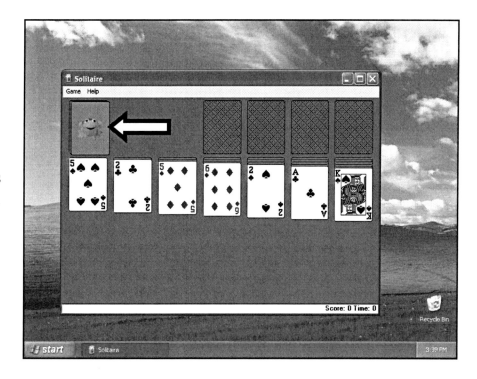

Section 9: Working with Multiple Windows

Multiple Windows

When you work with computers you are guaranteed to open up more than one window at a time.

? *Question:* Why would anyone open up more than one window at a time?

Answer: A good example would be my friend Ed. Ed loves to trade stocks. He gets on his computer everyday and checks out his stock reports. Each stock report is usually open in its own window. That way he can easily switch from one stock report to the next without losing any information.

Another good example would be my good friend Mary. Every morning she gets up and reads the newspaper on her computer and almost every morning she disagrees with at least one article in the newspaper. Without closing the window the newspaper is displayed in, Mary is able to open up a second window containing her Word Processing program. Using her word processing program, she writes her responses to the newspaper and easily references the newspaper for quotes. Since she can have multiple windows open at once, it is very easy to flip flop back and forth between the newspaper and the letter she is writing.

Active vs. In-active (on-top vs. behind)

Every time you open a program on your computer, it opens up in a window on your desktop. When you open up more than one window, the windows begin piling on top of each other. The window that is currently on top is referred to as the active window. All of the windows behind the active window are referred to as inactive windows.

Characteristics of the Active Window
- The window that is currently on top
- Blue title bar.
- Will have a light gray corresponding button on the task bar. (The button appears to be pushed in.)

Characteristics of the In-Active Window
- Any window behind the active window
- Light gray title bar
- Will have dark gray corresponding buttons on the task bar. (The buttons appear to be pushed out.)

Moving from One Window to Another

To activate a window, click its button on the task bar. This will bring the window you want to the front and all other open windows will be behind it. To bring a different window to the front, click on a different button on the task bar. You can flip-flop back and forth between windows by clicking on each button located on the task bar. To demonstrate, let's open up Solitaire. After you have opened up Solitaire, go back to your Start Menu and open up the program Notepad. The directions for opening both programs are below.

Opening Solitaire: Step by Step Instructions
1. Click on the START BUTTON
2. Highlight the option ALL PROGRAMS
3. Highlight the option GAMES
4. Highlight the option SOLITAIRE
5. Click on the option SOLITAIRE

Opening Notepad: Step by Step Instructions
1. Click on the START BUTTON
2. Highlight the option ALL PROGRAMS
3. Highlight the option ACCESSORIES
4. Highlight the option NOTEPAD
5. Click on the option NOTEPAD

Moving from One Window to Another: Visual Instructions

Only the
Solitaire
window is
open.

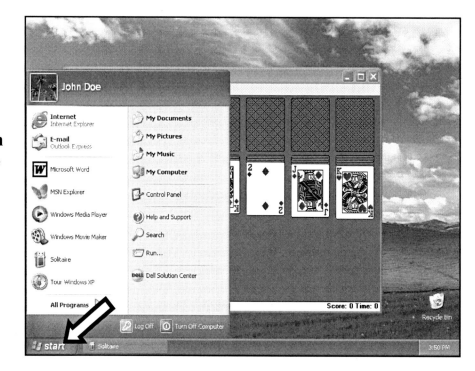

Click on the
START button
to open up the
Start menu.

Highlight the
option ALL
PROGRAMS.

Highlight the
option
ACCESSORIES

Highlight the
option
NOTEPAD

Click on the
option
NOTEPAD

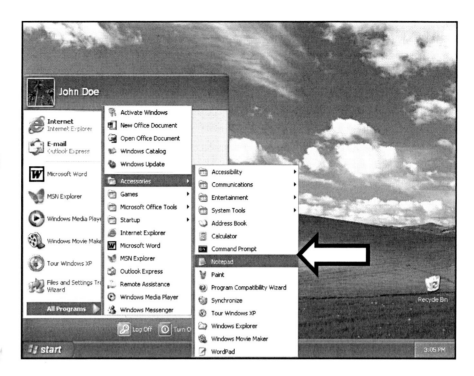

The Notepad
window will
open.

There are now
two separate
windows open.

The Notepad
window is on
top.

Notepad is our
Active Window.

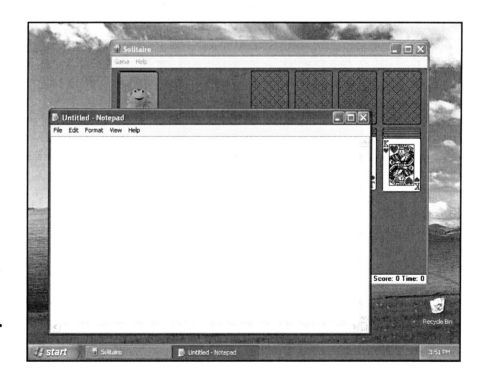

Switch between windows by using the buttons on the task bar.

Click on the SOLITAIRE Button.

Solitaire is now our Active Window.

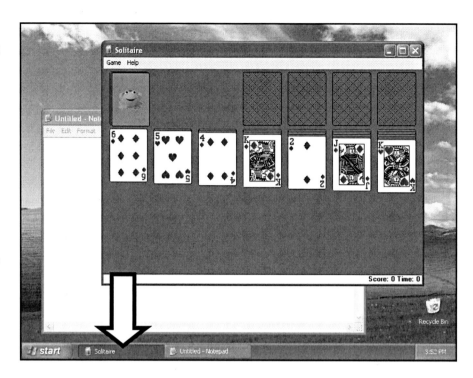

Switch between windows by using the buttons on the task bar.

Click on the NOTEPAD Button.

Notepad is now our Active Window.

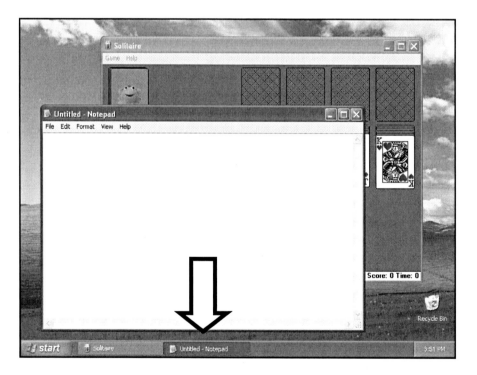

Switch between windows by using the buttons on the task bar.

Click on the SOLITAIRE Button.

Solitaire is now our Active Window.

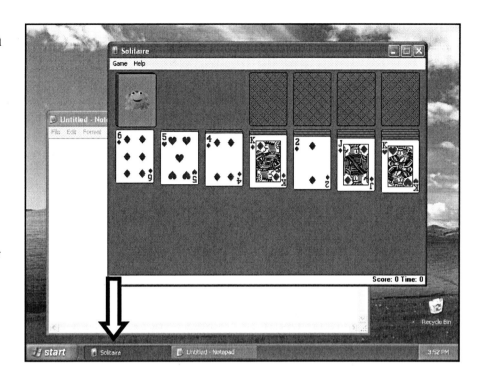

If you minimize a window, you will see what is behind it.

Click on the MINIMIZE button on the SOLITAIRE window.

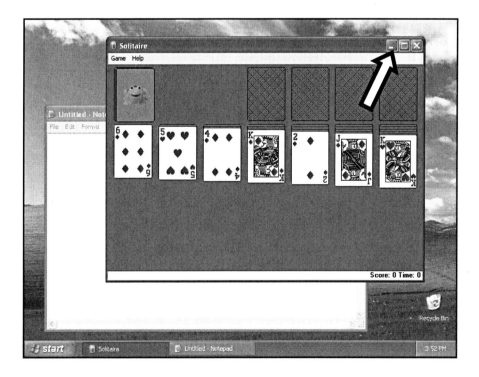

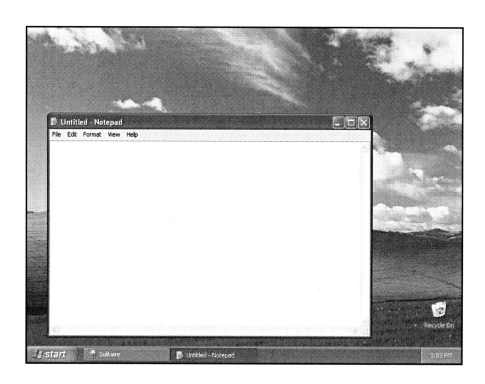

The
SOLITAIRE
window has
been
minimized.

Notepad is now
our active
window.

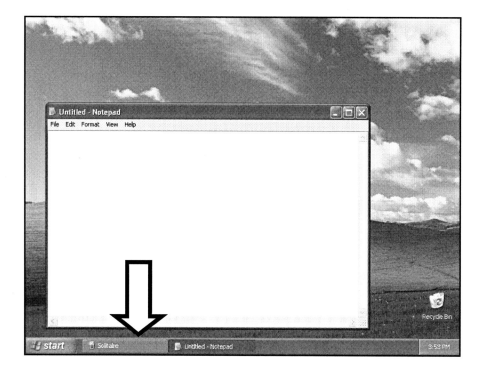

Click on the
SOLITAIRE
button.

The Solitaire window has returned to the desktop.

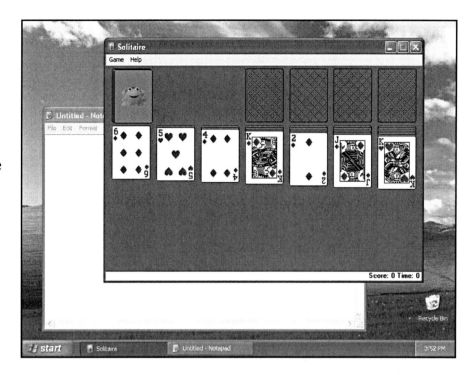

Closing the Correct Window

New computer users often close the wrong window when they are working with multiple windows. For example, let's say you are working with two windows, Notepad and Solitaire, and are about to win the game of Solitaire. Before you make your final moves in the game, you decide to close the Notepad window because you find it distracting. If you close the wrong window, you will end up closing your game of Solitaire and wiping out your card game. To avoid situations like these, you must realize that each window has its own separate set of minimize, maximize, and close buttons. If you have a difficult time figuring out which set of buttons goes with which window, simply follow the window's title bar to the right. The minimize, maximize, and close buttons will always be placed on the right hand side of that windows title bar. In the next visual example, notice how you have to close the Solitaire window and the Notepad window separately.

Closing the Correct Window: Visual Guide

Click on the "X" in the upper right hand corner of the Solitaire window.

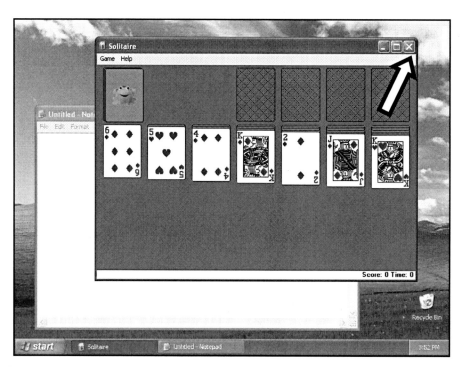

The Solitaire window has been closed.

Now close the Notepad window by clicking on the "X" in the upper right hand corner of the Notepad window.

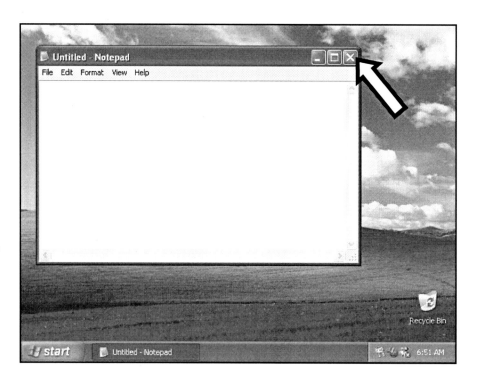

Both windows
have been
closed.

There are no
windows on the
desktop & no
buttons on the
task bar.

Chapter3: The ABC's of Windows

Chapter 4

Basic Skills

What You Will Learn in This Chapter
- ✓ How to move items on your computer by "clicking & dragging".
- ✓ The rules & objectives of Solitaire.
- ✓ How to use scroll bars.

Chapter 4: Basic Skills

Section 10: The Click and Drag

Clicking and Dragging

Clicking and dragging is a skill that allows you to move objects around your computer. A great way to learn to click and drag is to play the game of Solitaire on your computer. In order to play Solitaire, you need to be able to move the cards around the screen. You can move these cards by clicking and dragging. In order to move an object, place your mouse arrow on the object you want to move. While the arrow is on the object you want to move, press down the left mouse button and HOLD DOWN THE LEFT MOUSE BUTTON. DO NOT RELEASE THE LEFT MOUSE BUTTON. As long as you are holding down the left mouse button, the object the arrow had been placed on will move wherever you move the mouse arrow. When you reach your destination, release the object by removing your finger from the left mouse button.

Play a game of Solitaire. Each time you want to move a card, place your mouse arrow over the card, click and hold down the left mouse button, move the mouse arrow to your destination and then release the left mouse button.

Opening Solitaire: Visual Guide

Click on the START button

Highlight PROGRAMS

Highlight GAMES

Click on SOLITAIRE

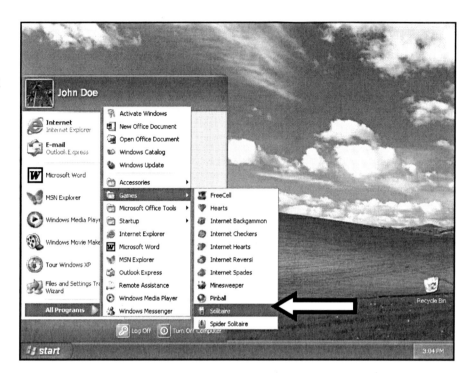

Step One: Place your mouse arrow over the object you want to move.

In this example, place your mouse arrow over the nine of spades.

Step Two:
Click the left
mouse button
and hold it
down.

While holding
the left mouse
button down,
move your
mouse arrow to
the destination.

The object will
follow

Step Three:
When you
arrive at the
destination,
release the left
mouse button.

The object will
be dropped.

The nine of
spades has
been moved on
top of the ten.

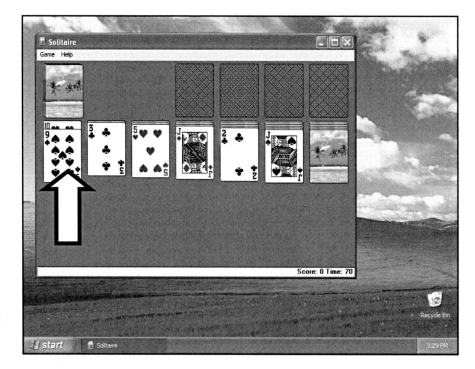

Chapter 4: Basic Skills

Section 11: How to Play Solitaire

Objectives

The object of Solitaire is to place all of your cards into four stacks of the same suit. These four stacks are placed in the upper right corner of the Solitaire screen. These four stacks must begin with Aces and go in ascending order. For example, an Ace would go first and then the two of the same suit, then the three of the same suit, then the four, and so on.

The seven stacks of cards across the middle of the screen are sorted through to get to the cards you need. You sort through the seven stacks of cards by moving the cards from stack to stack and creating rows of cards. These cards must be placed on top of each other in descending order and opposite color. For example, a red queen can be placed on a black king and then a black jack placed on the red queen and so on.

The stack of cards in the upper left hand corner of the screen is the deck. Every time you click on this deck, a new card is flipped over for you to try and play. If the card that flips over does not work, simply click on the deck again and another card will flip over. After you go through the deck once, a green circle will appear where the deck used to be. Click the green circle and the deck will be restacked.

Click on any card once to flip over the card.

Playing Solitaire: Visual Guide

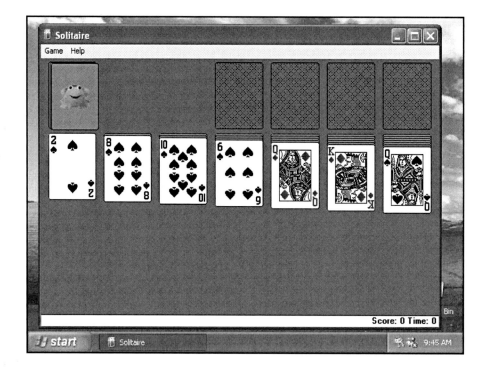

New game of solitaire

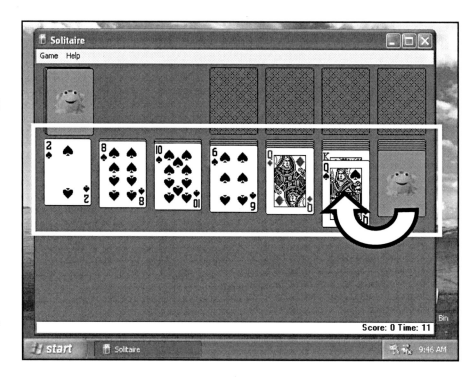

The middle row allows you to place cards on top of each other if they are opposite color and a lower suit.

The black queen fits on the black king.

Flip cards over by clicking the left mouse button on them once.

The black jack has been flipped over.

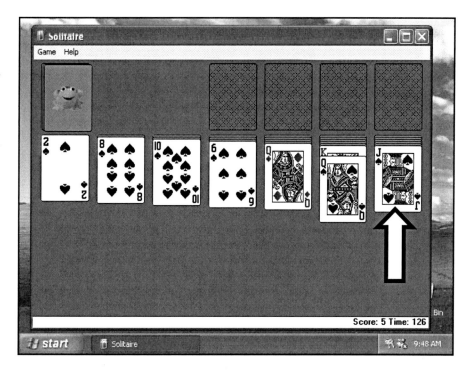

The black jack fits over the red queen.

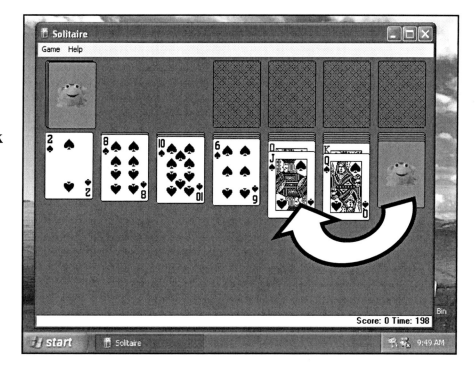

Flip cards over
by clicking the
left mouse
button on them
once.

The black ace
has been
flipped over.

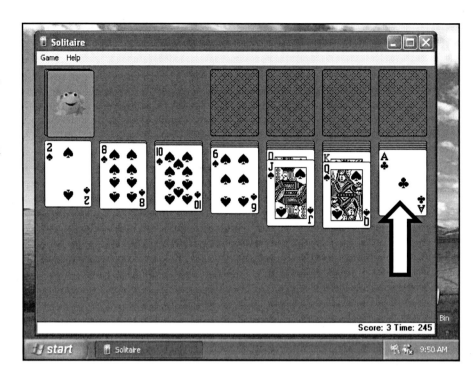

Aces should be
moved in the
four slots in the
upper right
corner.

The object is to
place all of
your cards in
the upper right
corner starting
with the aces.

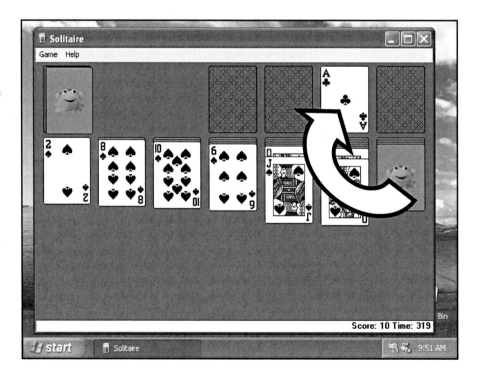

Your deck of extra cards is located in the upper left hand corner.

Click on the deck to flip over new cards.

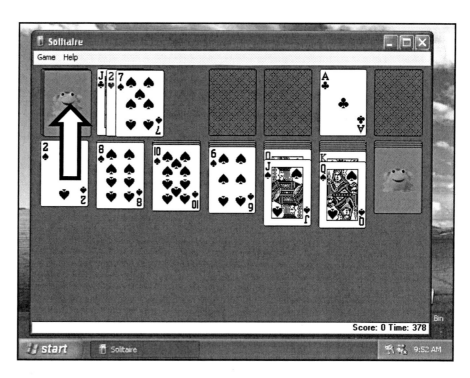

If you see a green zero you have flipped through the entire deck.

Click on the green zero to restack your deck.

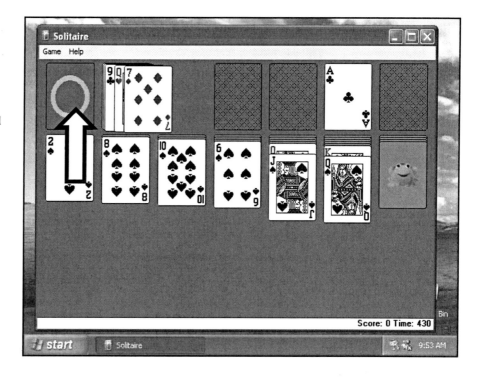

Rows are forming on the middle seven cards.

Aces are gathering in the upper right corner.

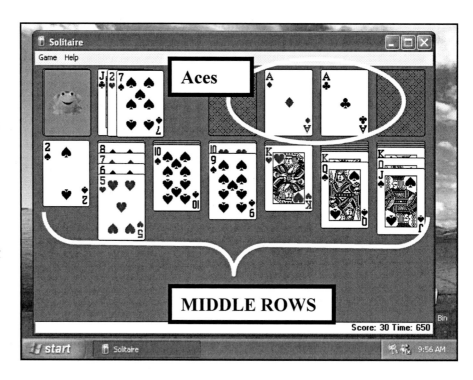

Rows continue to form as all aces are gathered in the upper right hand corner.

Once aces have been placed, cards of the SAME suit can be placed on top of them.

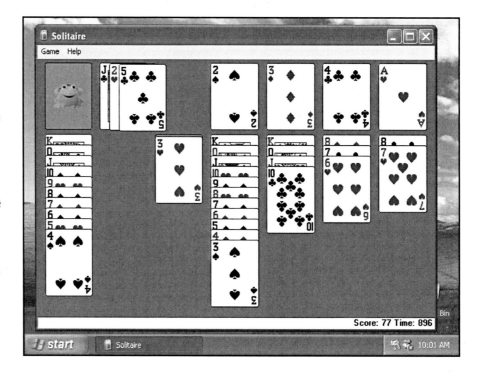

Section 12: Scrolling

Using Scroll Bars

The computer screen is similar to the scrolls used by the Ancient Egyptians. It is laid out in the same vertical fashion as the scrolls. This vertical layout sometimes causes information to be located above and/or below your the edge of your window. To see all the available information on the page, use the vertical scroll bar on the right side of the window screen.

The scroll bar is made up of an arrow pointing up, an arrow pointing down, and a light blue bar in the middle. Click on the up and down arrows at the top and bottom of the scroll bar to move through the information on your screen. Each click on the arrow pointing up will move your viewing screen one line up your document. Each click on the arrow pointing down will move your viewing screen one line down the document. The blue bar located within the scroll bar tells you where you are in relation to the total information available for viewing on the computer screen. If the blue bar is at the top of the scroll bar, you are at the beginning of the information. If the light blue bar is at the bottom of the scroll bar, you are at the end of the information. Notice, that when you press the up arrow, the blue bar will move up the screen. When you press the down arrow, the blue bar will move down the screen. If you press the up and down arrow and nothing happens, you may already be at the top or bottom of the document. To see if this is the case, check your blue bar. Is the blue bar at the top or bottom of the scroll bar?

Hint: Put your mouse arrow on either the up or down arrow and press and hold down the left mouse button. As long as you hold down the left mouse button, you will continue scrolling up/down your document. This comes in handy when scrolling through a long document.

Chapter 4: Basic Skills

Hint: Another way to scroll includes the "clicking and dragging" skill that you learned earlier. Place your mouse arrow on top of the light blue bar on the scroll bar. Press and hold down the left mouse button. While holding down the left mouse button, move your mouse arrow up and down the screen. By holding down the left mouse button, you will be able to "click and drag" the bar which will enable you to scroll through your document very quickly.

To practice using the scroll bar, you need to find a scroll bar on your computer.

Finding a Scroll Bar: Step by Step Instructions
1. **Click on the START button.**
2. **Click on the option HELP AND SUPPORT.**
   - **The HELP AND SUPPORT window will appear.**
   - **There will be a button at the top inside the Help window labeled INDEX**
3. **Click on INDEX**
   - **An entire list of help topics will appear on the left hand side of the Help window.**
   - **Because there are so many topics in the list, they don't all fit on the computer screen so a scroll bar is provided.**

Practice using your scroll bar here using the up and down arrows and clicking and dragging the dark gray bar. When you are finished practicing, close the window using the "X" in the upper right hand corner of the screen.

Finding a Scroll Bar: Visual Guide

Step One:
Click on the
START button.

Step Two:
Click on the
option
HELP AND
SUPPORT.

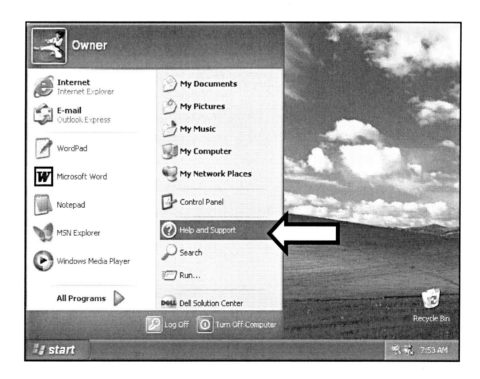

The HELP
AND
SUPPORT
window will
open.

Click on the
option
INDEX.

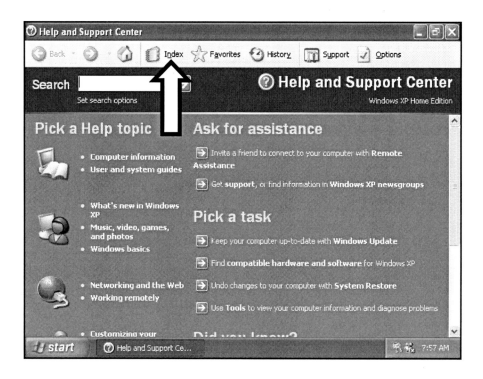

The Index of
help options
has so many
topics a scroll
bar is needed.

The scroll bar
has an up
arrow, a down
arrow and a
dark gray bar
in between the
arrows.

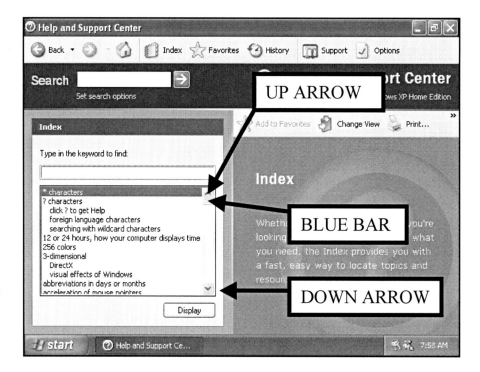

Practice moving through the list of topics using the scroll bar.

Click the up arrow to move up the list and the down arrow to move down the list.

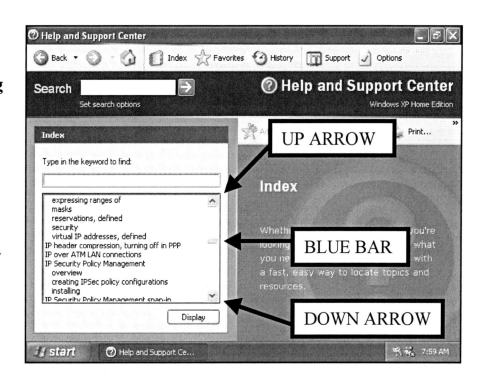

Once you are comfortable using the scroll bar, close the Help and Support Center by using the Close button (X) in the upper right corner of your screen.

Chapter 5

The Keyboard

What You Will Learn in This Chapter
✓ What the program Notepad is.
✓ How to open the program Notepad.
✓ How to use the blinking cursor.
✓ How to make corrections using the Backspace & Delete keys.
✓ How to move text down the screen & up the screen.
✓ The functions of the Shift, Caps Lock, Tab & Arrow Keys.

Chapter 5: The Keyboard

Section 13: Working with Notepad

What is Notepad?

You are now going to practice using the keyboard. This is not a typing class so don't worry if you type with one finger. Speed is not an issue when working with a computer. There are nearly 100 keys on a typical keyboard and, at first sight, the keyboard can seem overwhelming. It's not. In addition to the letter and number keys, about 90% of all basic word processing can be done with three additional keys. In this section, you will learn how to use these three important keys as well as many additional keys that make using the computer easier.

Before you can begin practice using your keyboards, you must first find a location on your computer that will allow you to type. You can find such a place by opening a word processing program on your computer. Word processing programs work together with keyboards to enable you to type letters, write stories, create lists, and much more. All in all, a word processing program is just a fancy typewriter. Most computers come with some word processing program already on the computer. You will be using a very basic word processing program called Notepad. Notepad comes on most computers. Don't worry if you don't have it on your computer. The lessons you will be reviewing can be performed on just about any word processing program.

Opening Notepad (a.k.a. the Typewriter)

To open notepad, you will follow similar steps to the ones you used to open Solitaire.

Opening Notepad: **Step by Step Instructions**
1. **Click on the START BUTTON**
2. **Highlight the option ALL PROGRAMS**
3. **Highlight the option ACCESSORIES**
4. **Highlight the option NOTEPAD**
5. **Click on the option NOTEPAD**

Opening Notepad: Visual Guide

Step One:
Click on the
START button.

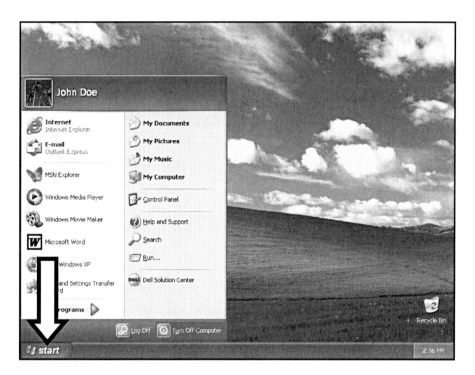

Step Two:
Click on the
option
PROGRAMS

Step Three:
Slide into the
Programs menu.

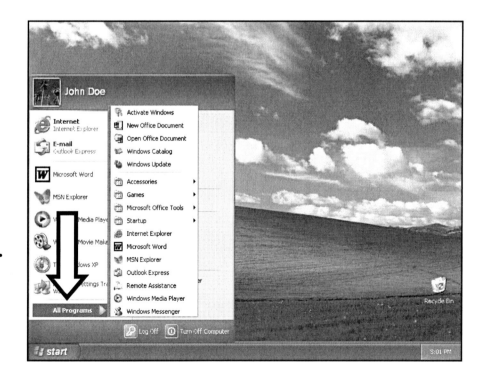

Step Four:
Highlight the option ACCESSORIES.

Step Five:
Slide into the Accessories menu.

Step Six:
Click on the option NOTEPAD.

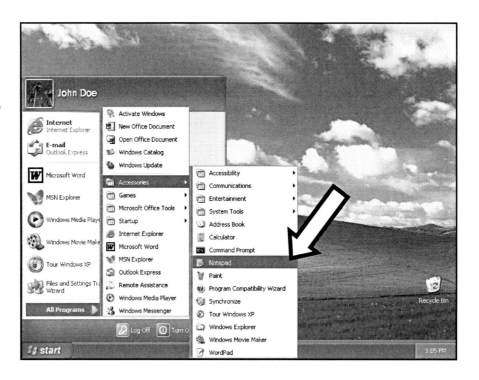

The Notepad window has been opened.

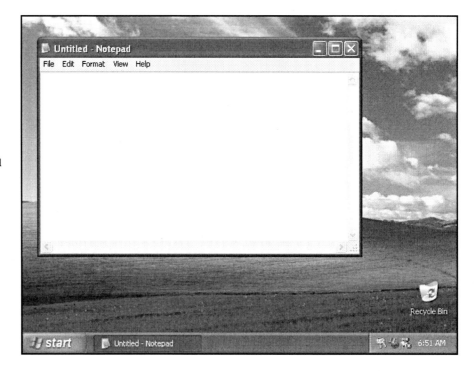

Time for Some Review:
You Already Know More Than You Think You Do!

Reviewing the Characteristics of Windows using Notepad

Let's take a look at the program Notepad. You may have never seen it before, but you already know quite a bit about it. The most important aspect to notice is that Notepad opened up in its own window. Remember, all programs open up in their own windows and all windows have the same basic characteristics. Let's test this theory. You have never seen notepad before and yet you should recognize the Title bar. The Title bar should read "Untitled-Notepad". Way to go Title bar. It's saying you opened up the right program. Secondly, you should recognize the three buttons in the upper right hand corner of the window -- the minimize, maximize and close buttons! Finally, take a look at your task bar. The task bar will have a button on it titled "Untitled". The name "Untitled" should match up with Notepad's Title bar "Untitled-Notepad". Amazing how much you already know about computers.

Reviewing your window characteristics.

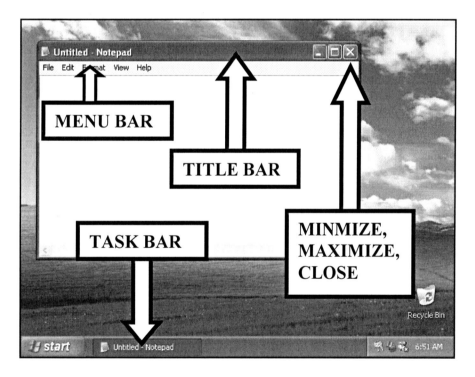

Chapter 5: The Keyboard

Section 14: The Blinking Cursor

What is the Blinking Cursor?

Let's explore a new topic. Move your mouse arrow around the computer screen and notice that, when the mouse arrow is placed above the white area on the notepad window, the mouse arrow turns into a capital letter "I". That capital letter "I" is still your mouse arrow. It does not change in any way except for the way it looks. I will always refer to the capital letter "I" as your mouse arrow. So why does the mouse arrow change form? It changes shape in order to tell you that you can type here. Whenever the mouse arrow turns into a capital letter "I," you know that you can type in the area beneath.

Now, look in the Notepad window. There should be a blinking line in the upper left hand corner of the window. We refer to this blinking line as the blinking cursor. If you do not see a blinking line in the upper left hand corner of your computer screen, simply place your mouse arrow anywhere on the white area in the Notepad window and press the left mouse button once. The blinking cursor will appear.

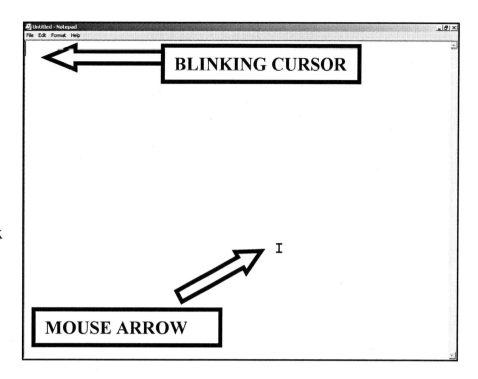

The blinking cursor will appear in the upper right hand corner.

Your mouse arrow will look like a capital letter "I".

The blinking cursor controls where you can type. If there is no blinking cursor you cannot type. One of the most frustrating aspects of computers can be learning about the blinking cursor. You must learn to look for it and get into the habit of always locating the blinking cursor before you begin typing.

To help look for the blinking cursor, try the following exercise. Click in the white area of the Notepad window to make sure you have a blinking cursor in the upper left hand corner of the screen. After you have located the blinking cursor, type the sentence "The quick brown fox jumps over the lazy dog." Don't worry if you make spelling mistakes. Just keep on typing. You can make corrections later. As you type, notice how the blinking cursor moves across the screen. When the blinking cursor comes to the end of the line, it automatically goes down to the next line. No carriage returns needed here!

Chapter 5: The Keyboard

Type the sample sentence and watch how the letters only appear where the blinking cursor is located.

Controlling the Blinking Cursor

Now, take your mouse arrow and click outside of your notepad window. If your window is maximized and is taking up the entire screen, make the window smaller by clicking on the maximize/restore button located in the upper right hand corner of the window. The maximize/restore button will be the middle button. After you have clicked outside of your notepad window, the blinking cursor will have disappeared. Try typing. Nothing happens because there is no longer a blinking cursor present on your screen. To get the blinking cursor back, take your mouse arrow and place it anywhere in the white area in the notepad window and click once. Notice that the blinking cursor reappears.

This brings me to my next point. You can control where the blinking cursor is by using your mouse arrow. Place your mouse arrow after the word "quick" in the sentence you just typed. Press the left mouse button one time. Notice that the blinking cursor appears where you clicked. Let's try that again. Place your mouse arrow after the word "brown" in your sentence and press the left mouse button one time. The blinking cursor, once again, appears where you clicked the left mouse button.

Understanding how to control the blinking cursor with the mouse arrow is an incredibly important concept to learn. One major reoccurring problem is that people assume the blinking cursor and the mouse arrow are one and the same. They are not. They are completely different. The mouse arrow controls the position of the blinking cursor. The blinking cursor controls where you can type.

Controlling the Blinking Cursor: Visual Guide

For our next example, the window cannot be maximized. If your window is maximized, as shown here, click the middle button in the upper right hand corner of the window to make the window smaller.

By clicking maximize/restore button, your window should now be approximately this size.

Click your
mouse arrow
anywhere
outside the
window.

The blinking
cursor will
disappear.

Without the
blinking cursor
we cannot type.

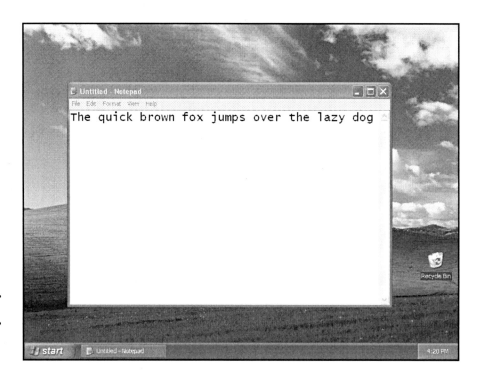

Place your
mouse arrow
after the word
"quick" and
click the left
mouse button
once.

The blinking
cursor will
appear
wherever you
click.

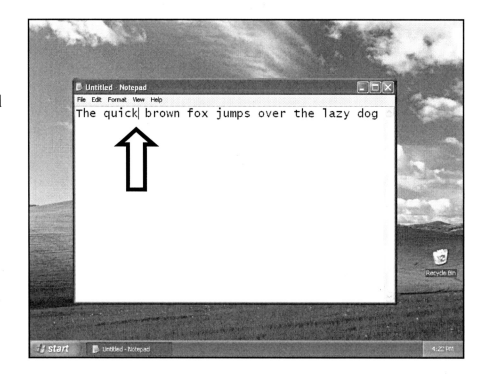

Try it again:

Place your mouse arrow after the word "brown" and click the left mouse button one time.

The blinking cursor will appear wherever you click.

Accidental Highlights

Sometimes when you click the left mouse button to change the position of the blinking cursor, a blue block will appear instead of the blinking cursor. If you get a blue block instead of the blinking cursor, it simply means that you moved your mouse as you clicked. This blue block is called a highlight, we will explain more about that in a later chapter. For now, if you get a blue block instead of a blinking cursor, simply start again. Place your mouse arrow where you want the blinking cursor to be and press the left mouse button one time. This time, be more careful not to move the mouse as you press the left mouse button. If you keep get a blue block every time you press the left mouse button, the problem may be that you are pressing too hard. Try clicking the left mouse button more gently.

CAUTION!

If you click and a blue square appears or some of your words become highlighted in blue, simply click again and the blue area will go away.

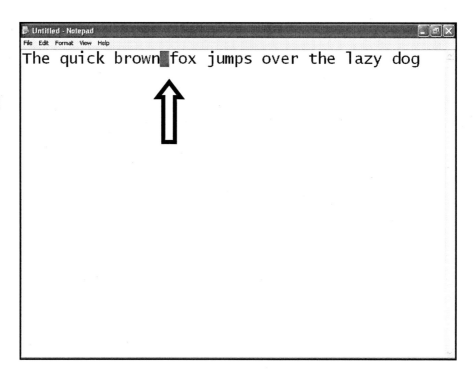

CAUTION!

Moving your mouse too much when you clicked caused this blue highlight.

Keep your mouse perfectly still when you click.

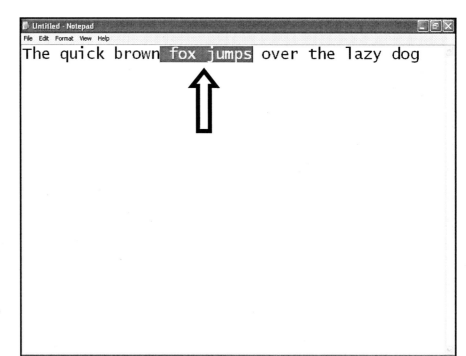

Section 15: Important Keys and Their Functions

The Backspace Key

The first key on the keyboard that I would like to introduce is the BACKSPACE key. The BACKSPACE key is located at the far right of the number line on the keyboard. Some keyboards will spell out the word BACKSPACE on the key while others will just use an arrow pointing to the left to symbolize the BACKSPACE key. The BACKSPACE key follows one rule. Every time you press the BACKSPACE key you will erase one space to the left of the blinking cursor.

To practice using the BACKSPACE key, take your mouse arrow and place it after the word "dog" in the sentence you typed. Click the left mouse button one time and the blinking cursor will appear where your mouse arrow had been placed. Hopefully, you now have the blinking cursor after the word "dog." If not, try again. Place the mouse arrow after the word "dog" and press the left mouse button one time. Once the blinking cursor is blinking just to the right of the word dog, press the BACKSPACE key three times. Each press of the BACKSPACE key will erase one space to the left of the blinking cursor or in this case the letters G-O-D will be erased. Let's replace the word "dog" with "cat;" simply type the word cat and it will appear where the word dog once was. Your sentence should now read "The quick brown fox jumps over the lazy cat". Your blinking cursor should be blinking just to the right of the word "cat."

The Backspace Key: Visual Guide

Step One:
Place your
mouse arrow
after the word
"dog" and click
the left mouse
button one
time.

The blinking
cursor will
appear after
the word
"dog."

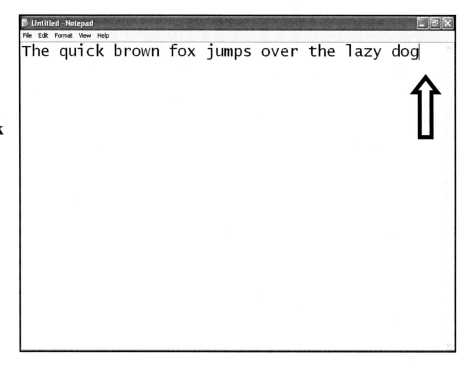

Step Two:
Press the
BACKSPACE
key three times
and the letters
G_O_D will be
erased.

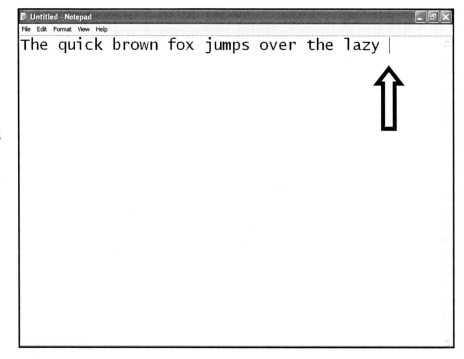

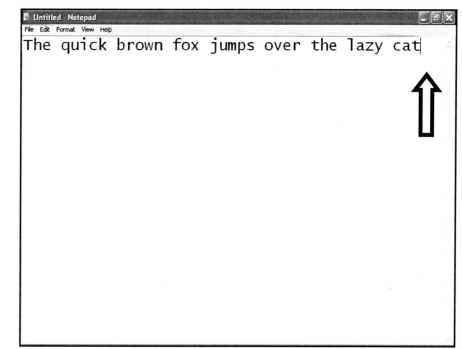

**Step Three:
Type the word
"cat."**

Let's try another one. Place your blinking cursor after the word "brown" in your sentence. Press the BACKSPACE key five times and the letters N-W-O-R-B will be erased. If this did not happen, your blinking cursor was in the wrong place. If this did not happen, review the rules of the blinking cursor on page 82 and try again.

Notice that after you erased the word brown, no empty space was left. The computer automatically moved the rest of the words in your sentence to fill in any would be empty space. Your sentence should now read "The quick fox jumps over the lazy cat" and your blinking cursor is somewhere between the words quick and fox. Let's make the fox a red fox. To do this, simply type the word "red". The computer will automatically make space for the word "red" to fit. You never have to make space for words. The computer will always make space for you. All you have to do is place your blinking cursor in the correct place and begin typing.

Step One:
Place the
mouse arrow
after the word
"brown" and
click the left
mouse button
one time.

The blinking
cursor will
appear after
the word
"brown."

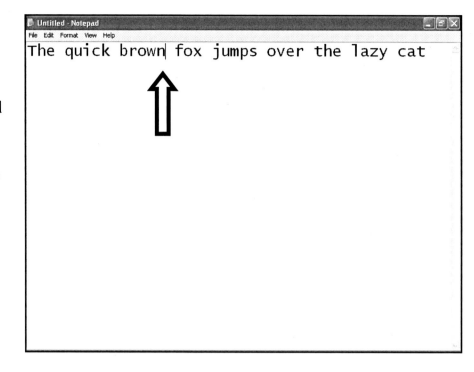

Step Two:
Press the
BACKSPACE
key five times
and the letters
N_W_O_R_B
will be erased.

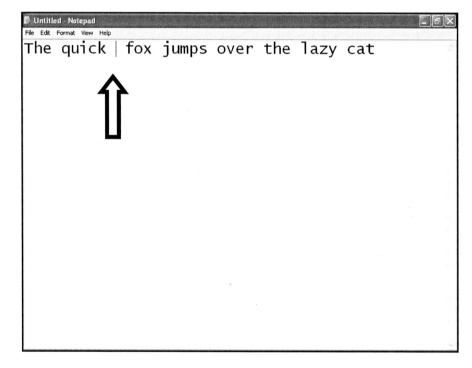

Step Three: Type the word "red."

The computer will automatically make space for the new word.

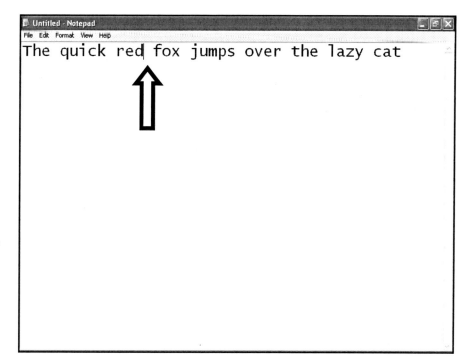

SOLUTIONS: When Words Run Together

Another common problem beginning computer users face is running words together. It is very common to see a sentence with words stuck together such as "The quickbrownfox jumps over the lazy dog." While the sentence is correct you forgot to put spaces in between the words. This can be easily fixed by placing your blinking cursor between the words that have been run together and pressing the space bar one time. In this case, take your mouse arrow and place it between the words "quick" and "brown." Press the left mouse button one time to call the blinking cursor to that position. Once the blinking cursor is between the words, press the space bar one time. You can follow the same steps to add a space between any words in your document.

Chapter 5: The Keyboard

WhenWordsRunTogether: Visual Guide

Step One:
Place your mouse arrow between two words that have been run together and click the left mouse button one time.

The blinking cursor will appear in between the two words

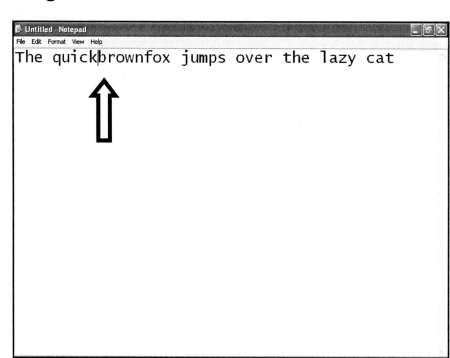

Step Two:
Press the space bar key and the words will be separated.

Second example: Place your mouse arrow between the two words and press the left mouse button one time.

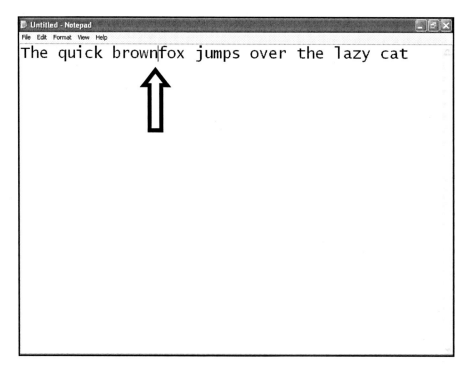

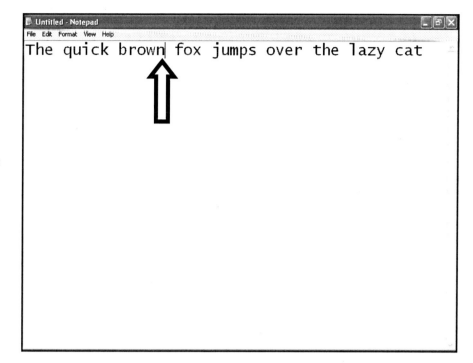

Example Two Continued:
Press the space bar key one time and the words will be separated.

Try making additional changes to your sentence. Try changing "quick" to "slow" and "lazy" to "black."

More Practice

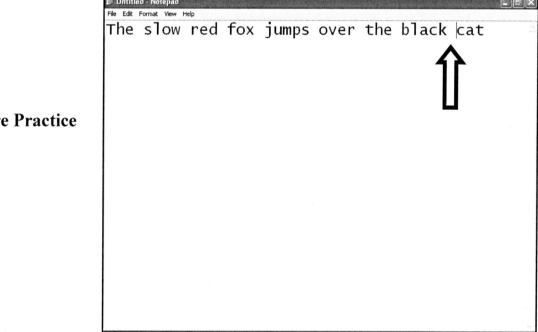

The Delete Key

The next key on the keyboard to introduce is the DELETE key. The DELETE key is usually found just to the right of the BACKSPACE key on the keyboard. The DELETE key's position may vary depending on the type of keyboard you are using. Sometimes the DELETE key has the entire word DELETE printed on it. Other times it may just read DEL. The DELETE key follows one simple rule. Each time you press the DELETE key, one space to the right of the blinking cursor will be erased.

Remember at this point, you should have the sentence "The slow red fox jumps over the black cat" typed in Notepad.

To practice using the DELETE key, take your mouse arrow and place it BEFORE the word "cat" in the sentence that you typed. Click the left mouse button one time and the blinking cursor will appear. Hopefully, you now have the blinking cursor BEFORE the word cat. If not, try again. Place the mouse arrow before the word "cat" and press the left mouse button one time. Once the blinking cursor is blinking just to the LEFT of the word "cat", press the DELETE key three times. Each press of the delete key will erase one space to the RIGHT of the blinking cursor or in this case the letters C-A-T will be erased.

Replace the word "cat" with "mouse". Simply type the word "mouse" and it will appear where the word "cat" once was. Your sentence should now read "The slow red fox jumps over the black mouse." Your blinking cursor should be blinking just to the right of the word "mouse."

The Delete Key: Visual Guide

Step One:
Place your
mouse arrow in
front of the
word "cat" and
press the
mouse button
one time.

The blinking
cursor will
appear in front
of the word
"cat".

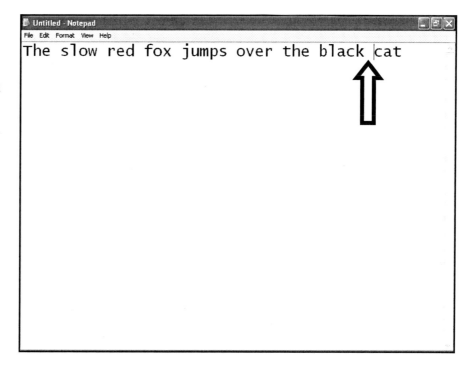

Step Two:
Press the
DELETE key
three times.
The letters
C_A_T will be
erased.

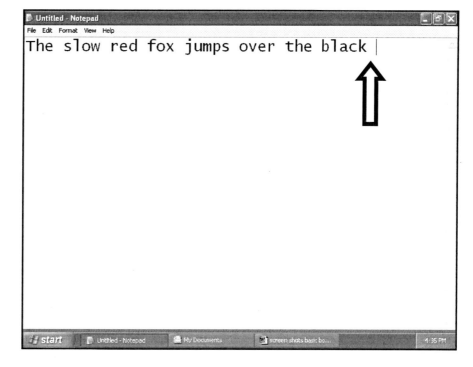

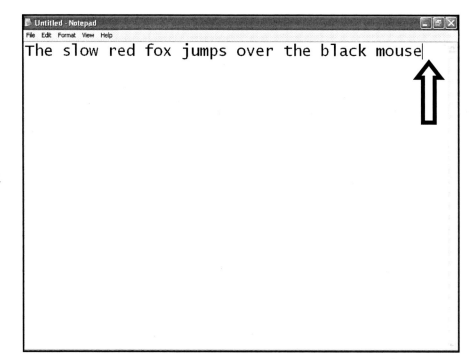

Step Three:
Type the word
"mouse."

Let's try another one. Place your blinking cursor BEFORE the word "red" in your sentence. Press the DELETE key three times and the letters R-E-D will be erased. If this did not happen, your blinking cursor was in the wrong place. If this did not happen, review the rules of the blinking cursor on page 82 and try again.

Notice that after you erased the word "red" no empty space was left. The computer automatically moved the rest of the words in your sentence to fill in any empty space. Your sentence should now read "The slow fox jumps over the black mouse" and your blinking cursor is somewhere between the words slow and fox. Let's make the fox a GRAY fox. To do this, simply type the word "gray". The computer will automatically make space for the word "gray" to fit. You never have to make space for words. The computer will always make space for you. All you have to do is place your blinking cursor in the correct place and begin typing.

Step One:
Place your mouse arrow in front of the word RED and press the mouse button one time.

The blinking cursor will appear in front of the word RED.

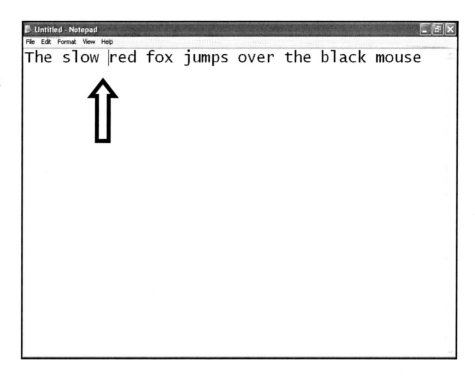

Step Two:
Press the DELETE key three times. The letters R_E_D will be erased.

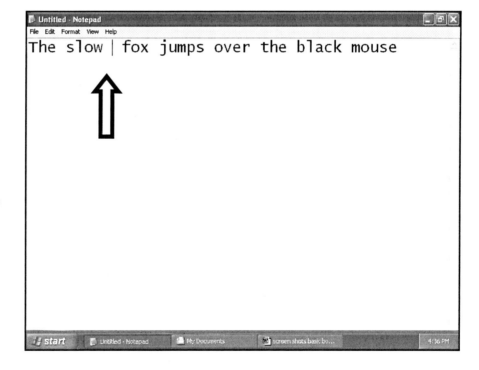

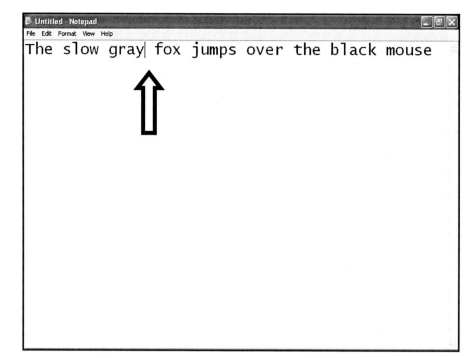

**Step Three:
Type the word
GRAY.**

Try making additional changes to your sentence. Try changing "SLOW" to "SMALL" and "BLACK" to "WHITE".

More Practice

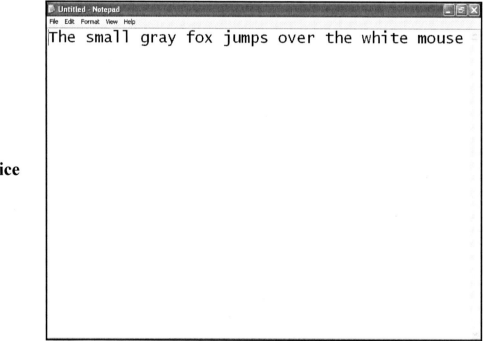

Chapter 5: The Keyboard

The Enter Key

The ENTER key is the next fundamental key you need to understand. The ENTER key follows one simple rule. When you press the ENTER key, the blinking cursor and everything to the RIGHT of the blinking cursor moves down one line. The ENTER key is most commonly used to insert blank lines in your documents, move your text down a page, and create spacing for new paragraphs.

If you are not following this book in chronological order, you will have to make sure that you have a word processing program such as Notepad open and have the sentence "The small gray fox jumps over the white mouse" typed.

We will examine how the ENTER key affects your text. In all cases, the ENTER key follows the same rule. The ENTER key will move the blinking cursor and anything to the right of the blinking cursor down one line.

Moving Text Down a Page

Place your blinking cursor in the upper left hand corner of your word processing screen. If you have been following along, the upper left hand corner of the screen will be by the word "The". Once the blinking cursor is in the upper left hand corner of the screen, press the ENTER key one time. What happened? The blinking cursor moved down one line and all of the text, that was to the RIGHT of the blinking cursor, also moved down one line. The ENTER key followed its rule and you were able to move your text down the screen.

**Step One:
Place the
mouse arrow in
the upper left
hand corner of
the screen and
click the left
mouse button
one time.**

**Your blinking
cursor will now
be just to the
left of the word
"THE".**

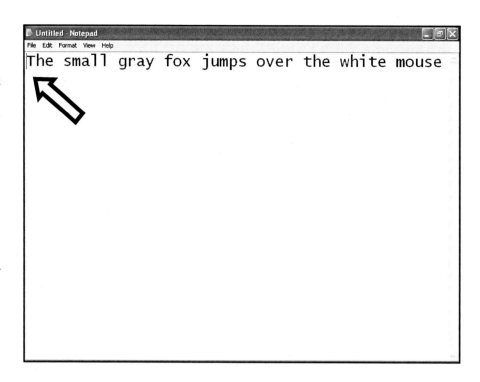

**Step Two:
Press the
ENTER key
one time. The
text to the right
of the blinking
cursor will be
moved down
one line.**

**Each press of
the ENTER
key will move
the text down
another line.**

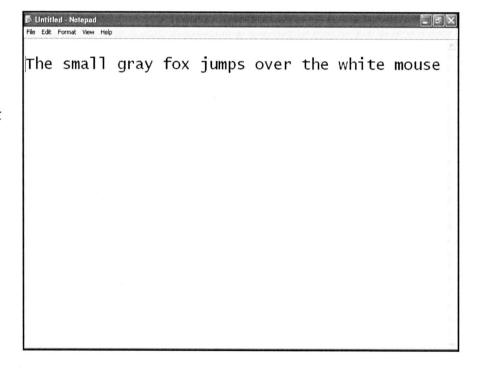

Creating New Paragraphs

Place your blinking cursor after the last word that you have typed. If you have
been following along, you will place your blinking cursor after the word
"MOUSE". When your blinking cursor has been placed after the word mouse

there should be nothing to the RIGHT of the blinking cursor. All of your text should be to the left of the blinking cursor. Press the ENTER key one time. What happened? The blinking cursor moved down one line, your text stayed where it was because it was to the LEFT of the blinking cursor and NO text moved down with the blinking cursor because nothing was to the RIGHT of it. Press the ENTER key again and the blinking cursor should move down another line. You have just created the spacing to begin a new paragraph. Type the words "New paragraph" and you will be able to see how your two sentences have been separated.

Step One: Place your mouse arrow after the word mouse. Click the left mouse button one time.

The blinking cursor will now be to the right of everything you have typed.

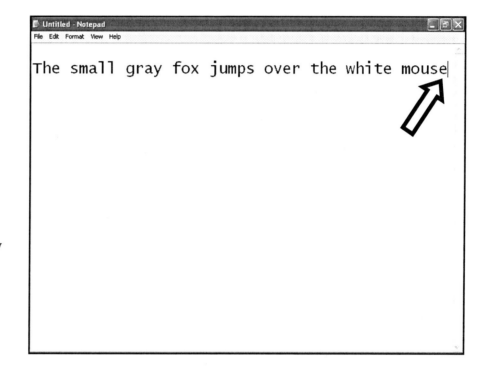

Step Two:
Press the
ENTER key
once. The
blinking cursor
will be moved
down one line.

Each press of
the ENTER
key will move
the blinking
cursor down
another line.

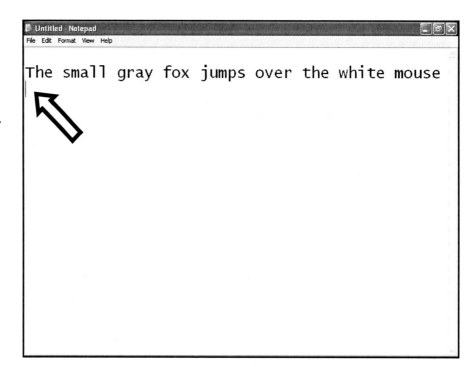

A new
paragraph has
been created.

Separating Text

Let's say that you have one big paragraph and you want to split it into two parts. You want to add a blank line in the middle of your writing. You can do this by placing the blinking cursor at the point where you want the split to occur. For example, if you want to split your sentence "The slow gray fox jumps over the white mouse" in half, you would place the blinking cursor between the words "fox" and "jumps". If you press the ENTER key one time all the text to the left of the blinking cursor, in this case, "The slow gray fox" would be unaffected. The text to the right of the blinking cursor "jumps over the white mouse" would be moved down one line.

In all three scenarios the ENTER key followed one simple rule: When you hit the ENTER key the blinking cursor and everything to the RIGHT of the blinking cursor moves down one line.

Step One: Place your mouse arrow in the middle of your sentence and click the left mouse button one time.

The blinking cursor will now have text on the left and right side.

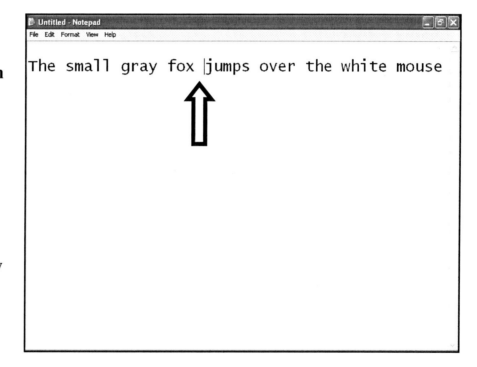

**Step Two:
Press the
ENTER key
one time.**

**The text to the
left of the
blinking cursor
is unaffected.**

**The text to the
right of the
blinking cursor
is moved down
one line.**

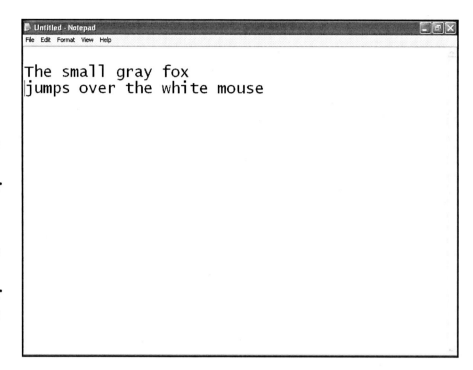

Moving Text Up the Screen

So far we have discussed moving text down the screen using the ENTER key but how do you move the text back up the screen. Let's take a look at this scenario with a brand new example sentence. If you have been following along, erase everything on your word processing screen by using your backspace key and/or your delete key.

Hint: When erasing large amounts of text hold down the DELETE key and everything to the right of the blinking cursor will erase very quickly. Hold down the BACKSPACE key and everything to the left of the blinking cursor will be erased very quickly.

Once everything has been erased type the sentence "The quick brown fox jumps over the lazy dog." Place your blinking cursor in front of the word "The" and press the ENTER key five times. This will move your sentence down five lines. Now, how do you move the sentence back up the screen? In order to move the sentence back up the screen you have to understand another simple rule of the computer. The computer does not see a difference between a blank space, letters, or numbers. All three of these items simply take up space and it is the computer's responsibility to keep track of these spaces.

In your current example you have a sentence and four blank lines above the sentence. In order to move the sentence back to the top of the screen you have to remove the blank lines that are located above the sentence. You can remove blank lines by using the DELETE key or the BACKSPACE key because these keys always follow the same rules no matter if you are erasing letters, numbers, or blank spaces.

Let's move your sentence back up to the top of the screen by using the DELETE key. First, as review, what does the DELETE key do? The DELETE key erases one space to the RIGHT of the blinking cursor each time you press it, therefore you need to place the blinking cursor in a position where the blank lines, that you want to remove, are to the right of the blinking cursor. In this first example, place the blinking cursor in the upper left hand corner of the word processing screen. Once the cursor has been placed n the upper left hand corner of the word processing screen, all of the blank lines are to its right. Press the DELETE key five times and the blank lines will be erased, moving the sentence back up to the top of the screen.

Moving Text Up the Screen: Visual Guide

Step One:
Type the sample
sentence.

Step Two:
Place your
blinking cursor
in front of the
word "THE".

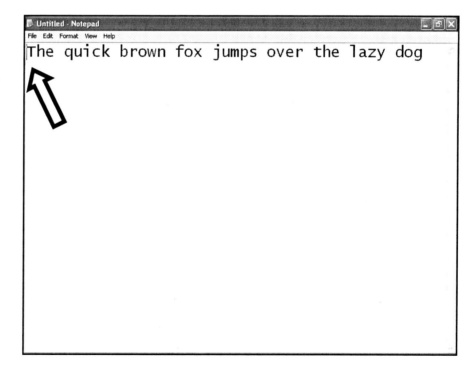

**Step Three:
Press the
ENTER key
five times.**

**The sentence
will move down
the page five
lines.**

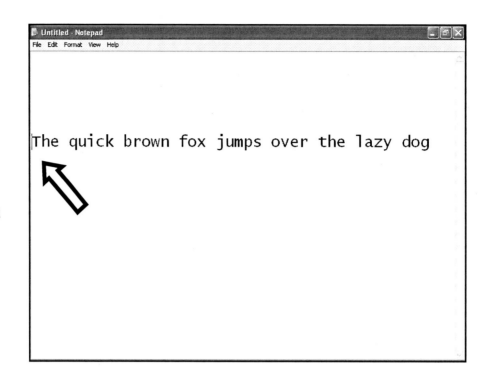

**Step Four:
Place your
blinking cursor
in the upper
left hand
corner.**

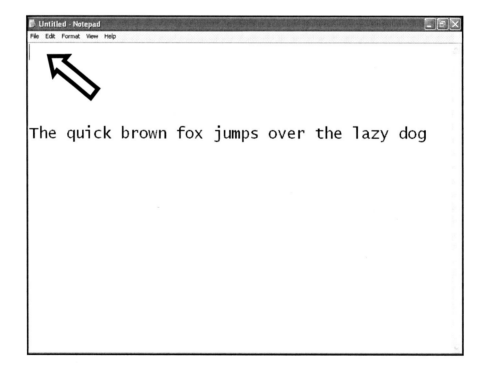

Chapter 5: The Keyboard

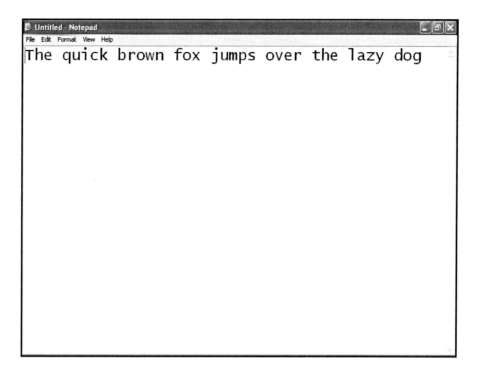

Step Five: Press the DELETE key five times. The sentence will move back to the top of the screen.

Let's move your sentence back up the screen using the BACKSPACE key. Before you try this approach make sure that you feel comfortable using the DELETE key to move text up a screen. We don't want to add any more confusion yet!

Place your blinking cursor in front of the word "The" and press the ENTER key five times. This will move your sentence down five lines. To move text up a screen using the BACKSPACE key you should first review the rule of the BACKSPACE key. The backspace key erases one space to the left of the blinking cursor so in this case you have to place the blinking cursor to the right of any blank spaces. How do you do that? Examine the situation. You have a sentence on your screen and four blank lines above it. You don't want to erase your sentence so place your blinking cursor at the very beginning of your sentence, before the word "The". Now your sentence is safe. It is to the right of the blinking cursor and you know that the BACKSPACE key only erases to the left of the blinking cursor. In this example, the blank lines are now to the left of the blinking cursor. Press the backspace key and watch your sentence move up one line each time you press the backspace key.

Step One:
Place the
blinking cursor
in front of the
word THE.

Step Two:
Press the
ENTER key
five times.

The sentence
will move down
the page five
lines.

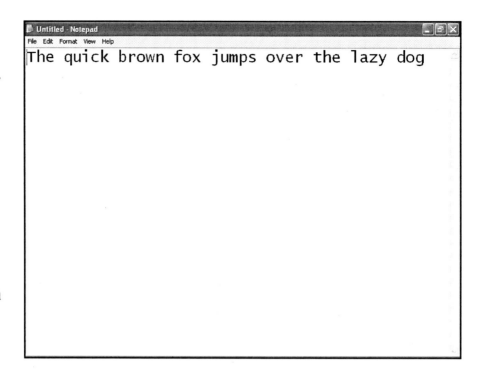

Step Three:
Press the
BACKSPACE
key five times.

The sentence
will move back
up the screen.

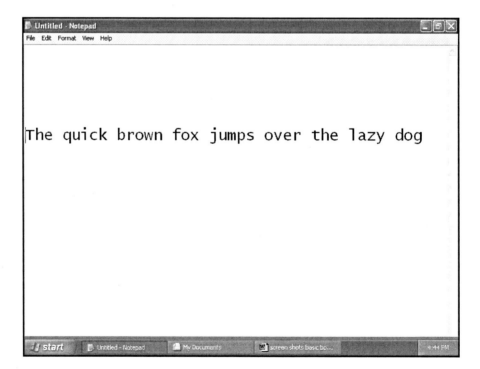

The Shift Key

The Shift Key on a computer is used in the same way as on a typewriter. If you want a capital letter, you have to hold down the shift key while pressing a letter on the keyboard. You will notice that there are two symbols on some keys. For example, take a look at the number line 1-9 and 0. Above each number is a symbol (! @ # $ % ^ & * ( )). To type one of these symbols you need to hold down the shift key and press the desired symbol. If the shift key is held down, the symbol will appear instead of the number.

The Tab Key

The Tab key is located on the left hand side of your keyboard. The tab key is used to help evenly space your work and indent new paragraphs. Each time you press the tab key eight blank spaces are inserted.

The Caps Lock Key

The Caps Lock key is located on the left hand side of your keyboard. If you press the caps lock key once, the caps lock function will be activated. All of the letters that you type will be capitalized. Press the caps lock key a second time and the caps lock function will be de-activated. Your typing will return to normal.

The caps lock key is important to be familiar with because of the common use of passwords on computers. Passwords are case sensitive meaning the password "watermelon" is not the same as "WATERMELON". If you have the caps lock key activated when you are typing a password, the computer will not accept your password. This can be a very frustrating experience so please remember to check if your caps lock key has been pressed if your computer won't accept your password.

The Arrow Keys

Normally set on the right hand side of the keyboard near the bottom is a set of four arrow keys. One points up, one points down and the other two point left and right. These arrow keys can be used to move the blinking cursor around the computer screen. They can be used as an alternative to using the mouse arrow to move the blinking cursor. Some people like to use them and some people don't. It's all a matter of preference. As you begin to use the computer more and more, you will probably begin to use both the arrow keys and the mouse arrow to move the blinking cursor.

So how do these arrow keys work? To demonstrate you will need to open a word processing program. If you have been following along, close your word processing program using the "X" in the upper right hand corner of the computer screen. When you close your word processing window a gray box will appear in the middle of your computer screen. This gray box is called a dialogue box because the computer is trying to ask you a question. Read this box. It will be asking you if you want to save the changes you made in your document. Click the NO button. See page 109 for visual example of the dialogue box. The issue of saving your work will be addressed later, beginning in Chapter 7. After you have successfully closed your word processing window, go back to your start menu and open Notepad or any other word processing program again. You want to start this demonstration from scratch. Once you have your word processor open, click your mouse arrow in the white area of the word processing window to start your blinking cursor.

The only item you should see on your word processing screen right now is the blinking cursor. Press the arrow keys. Notice that the blinking cursor doesn't move. Now type the sentence "The quick brown fox jumps over the lazy dog." Press your arrow keys again. Notice that the arrow keys will move the blinking cursor wherever you have typed. The arrow keys will NOT move the blinking cursor into areas where you have not typed. Because of this feature, the arrow keys are sometimes called the "shy" keys. They only let you go where you have already typed.

The Arrow Keys: Visual Guide

Example of a DIALOGUE BOX

Click the NO button.

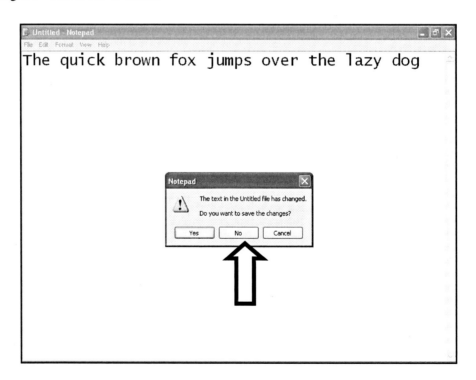

After clicking
NO, you will be
returned to
your desktop.

Step One:
Click on the
START button

Click on ALL
PROGRAMS

Highlight
ACCESSORIES

Click on
NOTEPAD

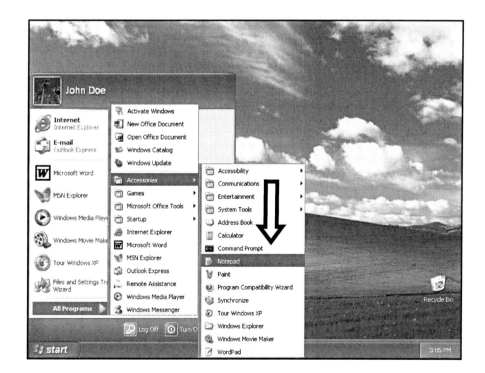

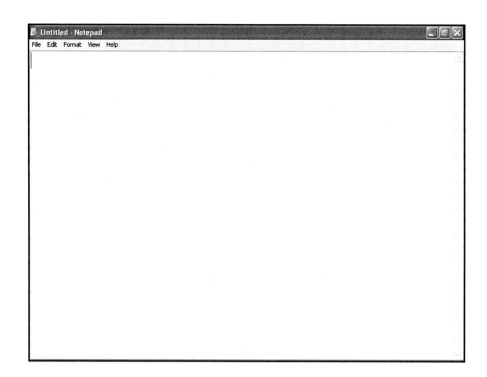

Step Two:
Press the
arrow keys
before typing
any letters.

The blinking
cursor will
NOT move.

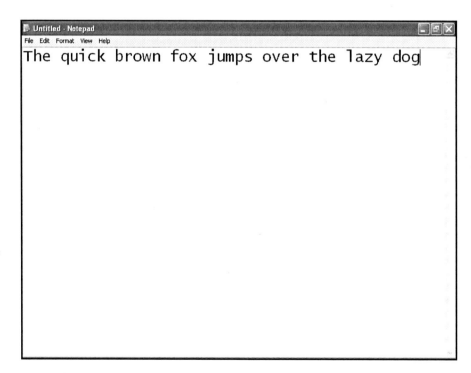

Step Three:
Type the
sample
sentence.

Step Four:
Press the
arrow keys to
move your
blinking cursor
throughout the
sentence.

Chapter 6

Successfully Navigating through the Computer

What You Will Learn in This Chapter
- ✓ What "My Computer" is.
- ✓ How to find files and other items stored on the computer.
- ✓ What the Back button is used for.
- ✓ How to locate your hard drive & what it's used for.
- ✓ How to locate your floppy disk drive & what it's used for.

Section 16: My Computer

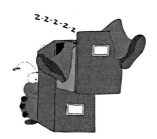

Introducing My Computer

In this chapter, we will discuss how your computer is organized. We will take a look at how to find items stored in the computer, how to store new items in the computer, and how to organize the items stored in the computer. In order to understand this chapter, you have to understand that computers are designed like filing cabinets. They have drawers, folders, and files. Computers follow the same rules as normal file cabinets.

Obviously the first step to successfully working with your computer's filing cabinet is being able to locate it. The computer's filing cabinet is located under the Start menu. Click on the START button one time and look for the option MY COMPUTER. Click on the option MY COMPUTER. "My Computer" contains all of the drawers in your filing cabinet. After you successfully click on the option "My Computer," a new window will open up with the title bar labeled "My Computer".

Time for Some Review:

You Already Know More Than You Think You Do!

Reviewing the Characteristics of Windows using My Computer

Before continuing with "my computer" let's review a few items. Even though you may have never even seen this window before you know a lot about it.

You know it has a title bar that tells you where you are and what you are looking at. In this window, the title bar is labeled "my computer".

You know that this window has a menu bar just below the title bar, which gives you options. You will use these menus later in this lesson.

You know how to use the minimize, maximize and close buttons located in the upper right hand corner of the screen.

You know there is a button located on your task bar labeled "My Computer" that corresponds with your "My computer" window.

Locating My Computer: A Visual Guide

**Step One:
Click on the
START button.**

**Step Two:
Click on
MY COMPUTER**

**It is found in the
Start Menu's
right hand
column.**

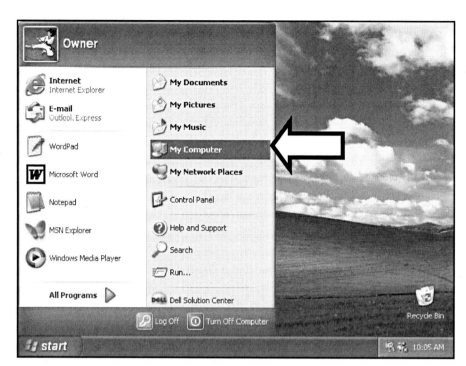

**The My
Computer
window**

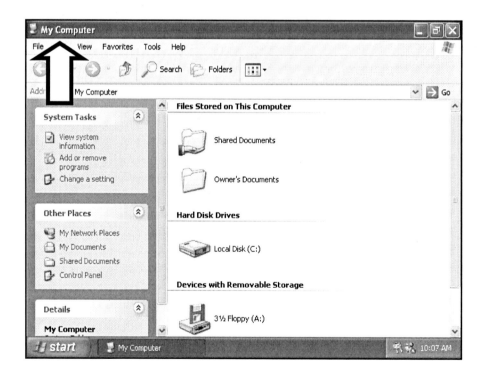

Do not worry if your computer screen looks slightly different in the following examples. The same concepts apply to all computers with XP.

So before you even begin, you know a lot about your window. Now, take a look at what the window contains. The window is divided into a left side and a

right side. You want to concentrate on the right side. The right side of the
My Computer window has three main categories. These three categories are
FILES STORED ON THIS COMPUTER, HARD DISK DRIVES and
DEVICES WITH REMOVABLE STORAGE. You may need to use your
scroll bar on the right hand side of the screen to see all three categories.

**The My
Computer
window is
divided into a
right side and a
left side.**

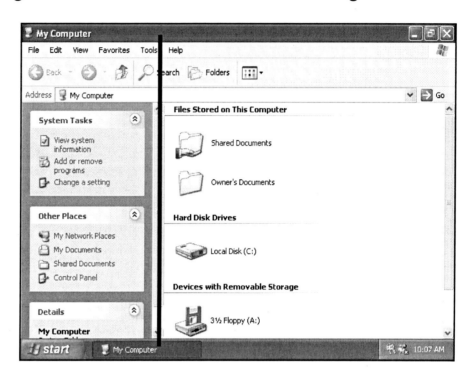

**If you cannot
see all the
options, you
may need to
click on the
down scroll bar
arrow to see
the rest of the
My Computer
window.**

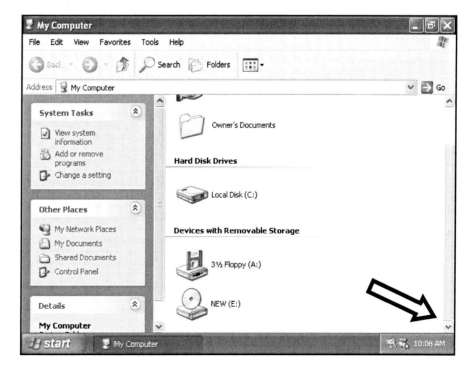

Section 17: Files Stored on this Computer

Introduction

The first category, FILES STORED ON THIS COMPUTER, contains folders in which you can store your information. There should be two folders under this first option. The first folder should be named SHARED DOCUMENTS. The second folder's name will depend on what user name you are logged in as. See Chapter 2, Section 4 for a further description of user names and logging in. The second folder is ALSO known as the MY DOCUMENTS folder. In the example that you will be using in this book the user name is "Owner" so the second folder is known as OWNER'S DOCUMENTS.

The Owner's Documents folder is the same as the My Documents folder.

The name of this folder is determined by your user name.

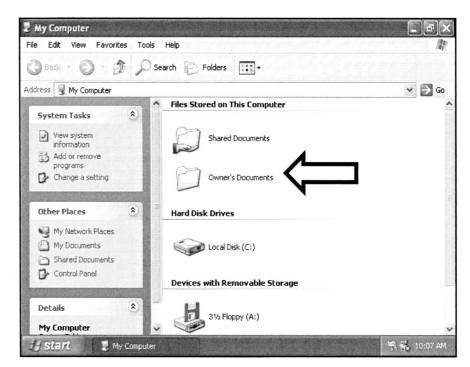

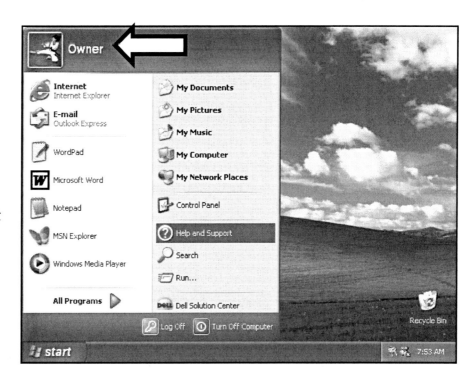

Your user name can be found at the top of the Start menu.

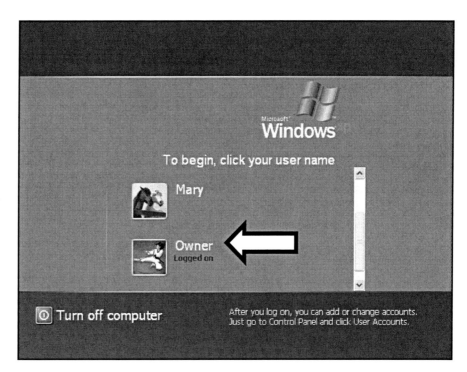

Your user name is chosen when you first turn your computer on.

This screen will only appear if you have created multiple user names.

Take a look at what folders you have located under your FILES STORED ON THIS COMPUTER category. What is your second folder named? Remember, this second folder is ALSO known as the MY DOCUMENTS folder.

Chapter 6: Successfully Navigating the Computer

Navigating through Folders

Open up one of your folders and see what is stored inside. In this example, open the OWNER'S DOCUMENTS folder. To open any folder on the computer, place your mouse arrow above the folder and double click. A successful double click will open the folder. You will know if you successfully double clicked because your title bar will change to the name of the folder you just opened. Take a look at the right side of the screen. It will contain any items stored inside the folder you just opened.

The computer helps you by automatically giving you two folders called MY MUSIC and MY PICTURES. The number of items stored inside your folders will vary depending on what has been stored on the computer in the past. If you are following along at home and you have many items stored in your folder, you or someone you know put them there.

REMINDER: Always double-check your title bar. It will always tell you where you are in the computer.

Navigating through Folders: Visual Guide

Step One: Place your mouse arrow on the picture of the "Owner's Documents" Folder and double click.

This will give you a look inside of the "Owner's Documents" Folder.

Remember: This folder is also known as your "My Documents" Folder.

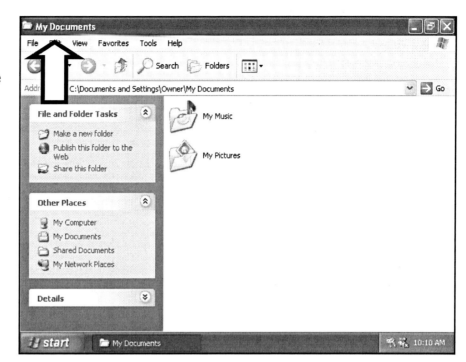

If you want to look inside any of these folders, simply place your mouse arrow on another folder and double click. The folder you clicked on will open up and its contents will be displayed. In this example, double click on the MY PICTURES folder to see what is stored inside. A successful double click reveals another folder named SAMPLE PICTURES. Double click on the SAMPLE PICTURES folder and several beautiful pictures will be revealed.

Remember, your computer is set up like a filing cabinet. So, if the computer is the filing cabinet, the My Documents folder is the top drawer of the filing cabinet, and My Pictures and My Music are folders inside of that drawer. To take our example farther, once you opened the My Pictures folder, you found a second folder inside of it called Sample Pictures and, inside of that folder, you found pictures which had been stored in the computer.

Section 18: The Back Button

Retracing your Steps

Before you take a closer look at any of these pictures, you need to be introduced to the BACK button, which is found in the upper left hand corner of the computer screen. The BACK button enables you to retrace your steps and is essential in making your navigation through your computer easy. If you click the BACK button, you will be returned to the previous screen. In this example you are currently looking inside the SAMPLE PICTURES folder. You know this because your title bar says SAMPLE PICTURES. If you click the BACK button one time, you will be returned to the MY PICTURES folder. Click the BACK button a second time and you will be returned to the screen previous to that, which was the MY DOCUMENTS folder. Click the BACK button again and you are returned all the way to the beginning of the example, MY COMPUTER. As you can see, the BACK button can come in pretty handy as you learn to navigate through your computer and all of its files.

Hint: Buttons turn light gray in color when, for some reason or other, they cannot be used. The BACK button will turn a light gray when you can no longer retrace your steps. In the previous example, the BACK button will turn a light gray when you are looking at the MY COMPUTER screen. The BACK button turns light gray and no longer works when you are on the MY COMPUTER screen because you cannot go back any farther. The MY COMPUTER screen was the first screen you opened. This concept applies to all buttons.

The Back Button: Visual Guide

Place your mouse arrow above the picture of the "My Pictures" Folder and double click.

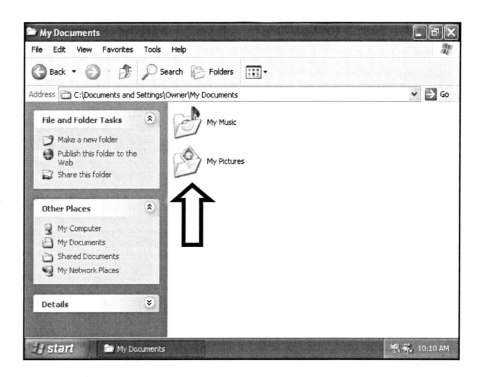

Place your mouse arrow above the picture of the "Sample Pictures" Folder and double click.

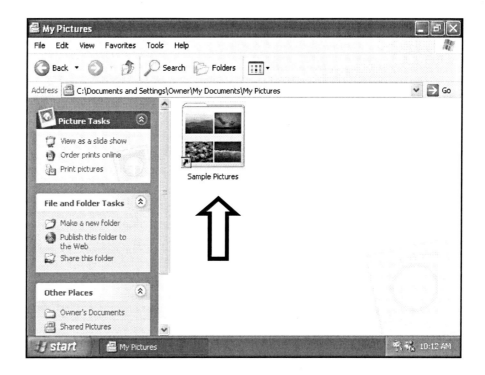

Look inside the "Sample Pictures" Folder.

Place your mouse arrow above the BACK button and click one time.

The BACK button retraces your steps.

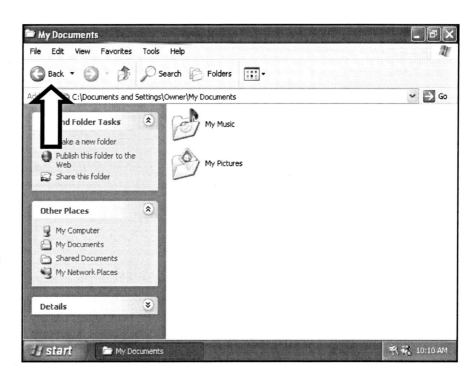

Place your mouse arrow above the BACK button and click one time.

The BACK button retraces your steps.

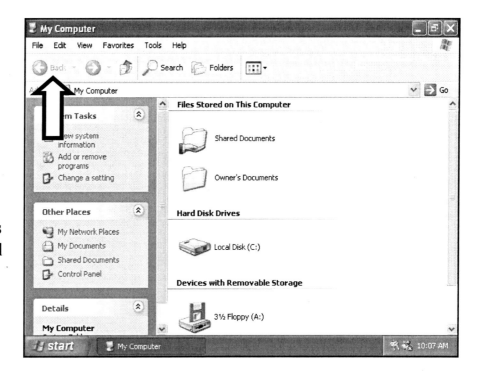

Place your mouse arrow above the BACK button and click one time.

The BACK button retraces your steps until you cannot go any farther back.

Go back to the SAMPLE PICTURES folder.
1. **Double click on OWNER'S DOCUMENTS (aka MY DOCUMENTS)**
2. **Double click on MY PICTURES,**
3. **Double click on SAMPLE PICTURES.**

You should be looking inside the SAMPLE PICTURES folder now. To take a closer look at one of the sample pictures, you need to double click it. In this example you will double click the picture SUNSET. After a successful double click, the picture SUNSET will open up in its very own window. Make note of this. Whenever you double click to open a <u>folder,</u> you keep working with the same window. In this example you viewed the contents of MY COMPUTER, OWNER'S DOCUMENTS, MY PICTURES, and SAMPLE PICTURES all within the same window. You never had more than one window open.

Whenever you double click to open a <u>file</u> (i.e picture, letter, recipe, etc.), that file will open up in its own window. With this concept in mind let's take a look at this example in more detail. SAMPLE PICTURES is in the background and SUNSET is in front. Both windows have a separate title bar, separate minimize, maximize, and close buttons. They also have separate buttons on the task bar. These windows will work completely independently of each other. You can either work with the SUNSET window or go back to SAMPLE PICTURES and continue working with its contents.

Opening a File: Visual Guide

Look inside the "Sample Pictures" Folder.

Place your mouse arrow on the picture of the Sunset and double click.

The picture of the Sunset will open in its own window.

We now have two separate windows open.

REMINDER: When working with more than one window you can switch back and forth between the two windows by clicking on the windows' corresponding button on the task bar.

You can move
back and forth
between
windows by
clicking on the
task bar
buttons

Click on the
SAMPLE
PICTURES
button.

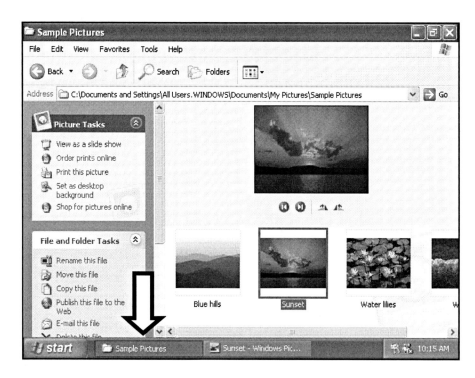

Click on the
SUNSET
button.

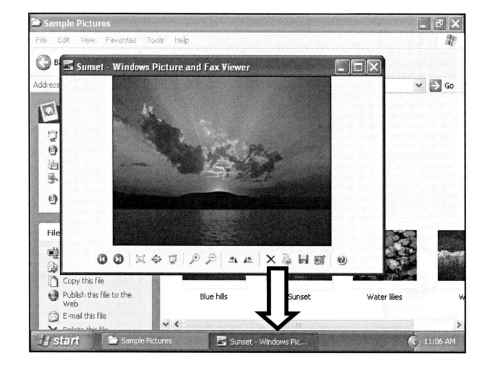

Click on the SAMPLE PICTURES button.

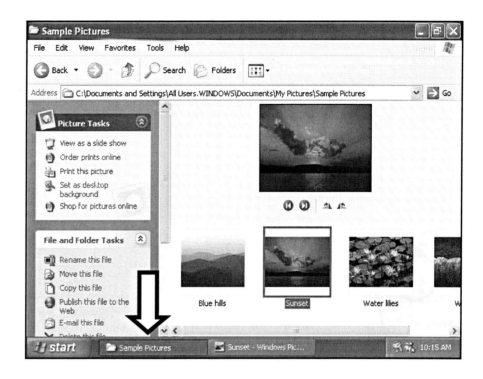

You can apply these concepts to nearly all computers. Do not be afraid to look through your computer and its files. Actually, it is good practice. Double click on folders to see what is inside of them and then use the back button to retrace your steps. When you are finished looking through your computer, simply click the "X" in the upper right hand corner of your screen to close any windows that you have opened.

Section 19: Hard Disk Drives

Introduction

Remember when we started Chapter 7? We began by looking at the My Computer window. The first category we looked at was FILES STORED ON THE COMPUTER. Now let's look at the second category: HARD DISK DRIVES. HARD DISK DRIVES contains a drawer named Local Disk (C:). The Local Disk (C:) drawer contains all the computer's information and

131

storage. Until you feel comfortable using the computer, you do not need to open this drawer.

NOTE: In computer terms "drawers" are also know as "drives". These two terms can be used interchangeably.

Section 20: Devices with Removable Storage

Introduction

The third category, DEVICES WITH REMOVABLE STORAGE, contains all of the drawers (drives) that allow you to *access* information stored on items such as floppy disks and CDs. These devices also enable you to *store* information outside of the computer on some type of external media such as a floppy disk or CD. In order to access information in any of these drawers you first need to insert the floppy disk or CD into your computer. After inserting the floppy disk or CD into your computer, you would double click on the corresponding drawer, i.e 3 ½ Floppy (A:) for a floppy disk, to access the information stored on that floppy disk.

HINT: Look at the pictures next to each item in your MY COMPUTER WINDOW. The pictures will help you figure out what each item represents. For example, the 3 ½ Floppy (A:) drawer should have a picture of a floppy disk next to it and the CD ROM, usually drive (E:) or (F:), should have a picture of a CD next to it.

The DEVICES WITH REMOVABLE STORAGE category is located at the bottom of the My Computer window.

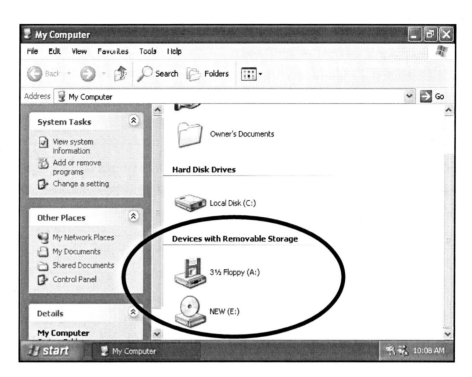

In this example, take a look at the contents of a floppy disk. In order to start from scratch, please close any open windows by clicking on the "X" in the upper right hand corner. After all windows are closed, open up MY COMPUTER.

Quick reference: Steps to Open MY COMPUTER
1. **Click on the START Menu**
2. **Click on the option MY COMPUTER**

Floppy Disk Drive: 3 ½ floppy (A:)
The "A" drawer, 3 ½ floppy (A:), or "A" drive, enables you to see information stored on floppy disks. To check what information is stored on a floppy disk, you first need to place a floppy disk into the computer via the floppy disk drive. After the floppy disk has been inserted into the floppy disk drive, you can place your mouse arrow on top of the "A" drive icon and double click the left mouse button. The contents of the "A" drive will be shown to you in its own window. To check to make sure that you have successfully accessed your "A" drive, check the title bar of the windows you have open. If it says 3 ½ floppy (A:) or "A" drive you have been successful in opening up your "A" drive. You should also check your task bar at the bottom of your screen. Remember, every window you open will have a corresponding button on the task bar. When you have successfully opened your "A" drive, there will be a button on your task bar labeled "3 ½ Floppy (A:).

Chapter 6: Successfully Navigating the Computer

REMINDER: It is a good habit to always check your task bar to see how many windows you have open.

The opened "A" drive window will display whatever information is located on the currently inserted floppy disk. The information will be displayed as icons (pictures) with each item being represented by its own icon (picture). To access any of these items, place your mouse arrow on the item you want to look at (open) and double click the left mouse button. When you have successfully opened the desired icon, the item will be displayed in its own window. Remember, the window's title bar and corresponding button on the task bar will display the name of the opened icon. You will now have two windows open, the "A" drive window, and the opened item's window. Each window will work completely independently of the other. You may minimize, maximize, close, or work with each one separately from the other.
When you are done working with either window, simply click the "X" in the upper right corner of the window you want to close and the window will disappear from the screen. The corresponding button in the task bar will also disappear.

If you wish to take a look at the contents of another floppy disk, you will need to first retrace your steps. In the upper left hand corner of your computer screen will be a button labeled BACK with an arrow pointing to the left. Place you mouse arrow on top of this button and click the left mouse button one time. The back button will take you back one screen each time you press it. If you are looking at your "A" drive, clicking the BACK button one time will take you back to the MY COMPUTER screen. If you get lost, check your title bar and your task bar to see where you are. Once you are back to the MY COMPUTER screen, remove the floppy disk from the floppy disk drive. To do so, there is usually a small lever to press by the opening of the floppy disk drive. Press that button and the floppy disk should pop out. After you remove the floppy disk, you can view the contents of another floppy disk by inserting the new floppy disk into the floppy disk drive and repeating the previous steps.

In this book you will only deal with basic computer skills. You will learn to store and organize your work on your computer and to a floppy disk using the MY COMPUTER window.

The Floppy Disk Drive: Visual Guide

Step One: Place your mouse arrow on the START button. Click the left mouse button one time.

Step Two: Click on the option MY COMPUTER

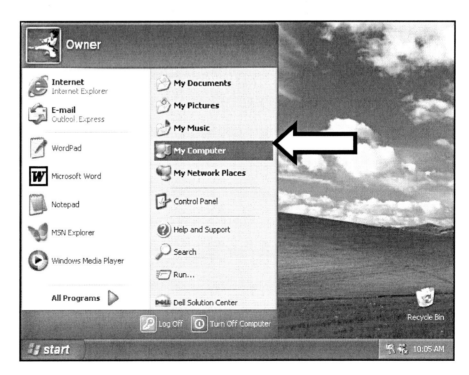

Step Three: Place a floppy disk into the floppy disk drive.

Step Four: Double click the 3 ½ Floppy (A:) Drive.

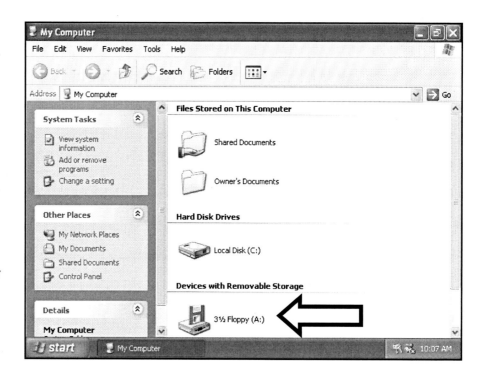

Take a look at the contents of the floppy disk.

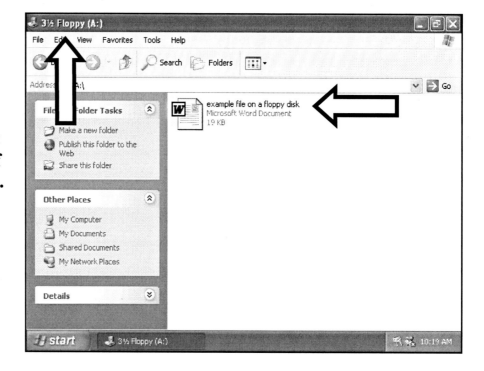

REMEMBER:
You can retrace your steps by clicking the BACK button.

Clicking the BACK button at this screen will return you to the My Computer window.

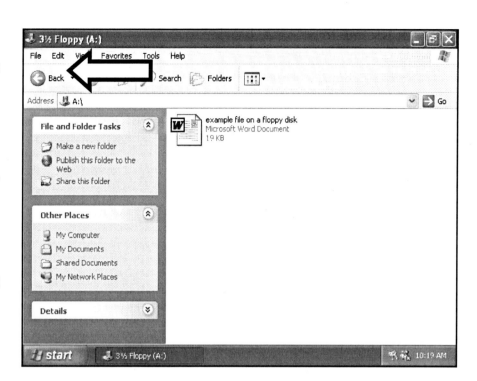

Chapter 6: Successfully Navigating the Computer

Chapter 7

Saving Your Work

What You Will Learn in This Chapter
- ✓ The definition of the word "save."
- ✓ How to use the program Notepad to create a grocery list.
- ✓ How to save a document, such as our grocery list, to the computer.
- ✓ How to find something on your computer once you have saved it.
- ✓ The difference between "Save" & "Save As."
- ✓ How to save a document to a floppy disk.
- ✓ How to access information stored on a floppy disk.
- ✓ How to "Back-Up" files to a floppy disk.

Chapter 7: Saving Your Work

Section 21: The Concept of Saving

What is Saving?

"Saving" is the process of telling the computer to remember something. When you save your work, you tell the computer to remember something permanently. Any information you do not save will be lost when the computer or the program you are working on is shut down.

The concept of "saving" can be best described through example. If you are typing a letter and the electricity goes out, shutting your computer off, when you turn the computer back on, the letter that you were working on will be gone. You will have to start over. If you saved your work previous to the power going out, when you turn your computer back on, your letter will be safely stored unchanged in whatever location you had placed it during the "saving process". For this reason, it is very important to save your work frequently. The "saving process" is discussed in the following pages.

Chapter 7: Saving Your Work

Examples of Saving: Visual Guide

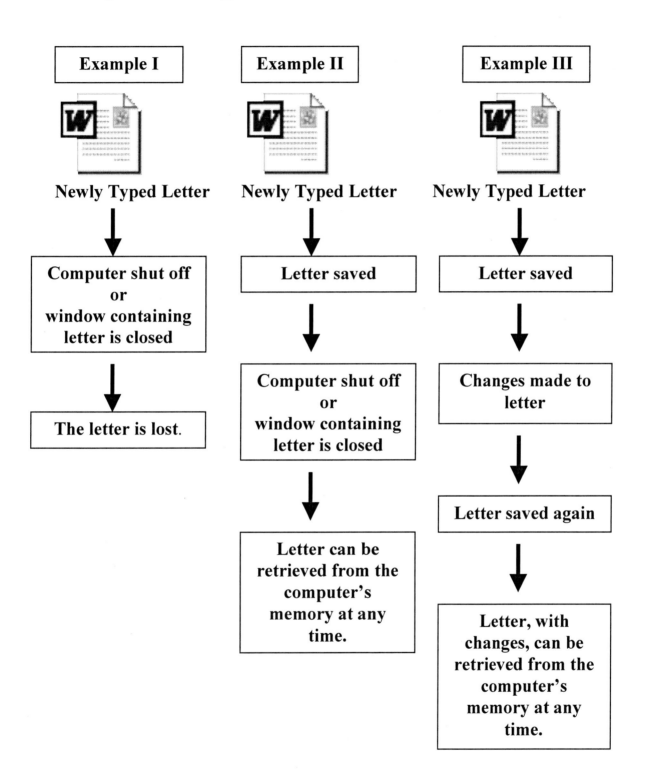

Example I	Example II	Example III

Newly Typed Letter   Newly Typed Letter   Newly Typed Letter

Example I
- Computer shut off or window containing letter is closed
- The letter is lost.

Example II
- Letter saved
- Computer shut off or window containing letter is closed
- Letter can be retrieved from the computer's memory at any time.

Example III
- Letter saved
- Changes made to letter
- Letter saved again
- Letter, with changes, can be retrieved from the computer's memory at any time.

Chapter 7: Saving Your Work

To help understand the concept of saving, you should compare your computer to working with a traditional filing cabinet. Everyone knows how to use a filing cabinet and the concepts are pretty much the same. Filing cabinets have drawers and inside those drawers are folders. You use these folders to help organize your work and keep the drawers looking neat. Computers are organized in the same fashion.

You are going to create and save a very important grocery list. Doing this will give you experience and teach you how your computer is organized. To type up this grocery list you will need to use a word processing program. After you type up the grocery list using the word processing program Notepad, you can store (save) that grocery list on the computer's desktop, on the computer's hard drive, which is similar to a filing cabinet, or store (save) the list on a floppy disk, which is similar to a brief case.

Section 22: Creating a Document: The Grocery List

Opening Notepad
1. Click on the START button in the lower left hand corner of your desktop.
2. Slide your mouse arrow onto the option: ALL PROGRAMS
3. After a moment, all the programs on your computer will be displayed in a submenu, which will be displayed to the right.
4. Slide your mouse arrow into the programs submenu. Remember, in order to move your mouse arrow into any submenu, you have to slide your mouse arrow directly into the submenu without leaving the blue highlighted area.

5. After your mouse arrow has slid into the programs submenu, move your mouse arrow to the option ACCESSORIES. When the mouse arrow is on Accessories, Accessories will become highlighted and the accessories submenu will appear.

6. Slide your mouse arrow into the accessories menu.

7. After your mouse arrow has slid into the Accessories submenu, move your mouse arrow to the option NOTEPAD. When your mouse arrow is above Notepad, Notepad will be highlighted in blue.

8. Click your left mouse button once. The word processing program Notepad will open.

Making your Grocery List

Look in the upper left hand corner of the Notepad window. The blinking cursor should be there. If the blinking cursor is not present in the notepad window, click your left mouse button anywhere inside the notepad window. The blinking cursor will appear.

REMINDER: Remember, Chapter 5: Section 14 explained how the blinking cursor controls where you can type. If the blinking cursor is not present, you cannot type.

Let's put milk, eggs, and cheese into our grocery list. Type these words into your notepad window. After you type each word, press the ENTER key on your keyboard. This will move your blinking cursor down to the next line.

After you type in milk, eggs, and cheese you want to save your work. If you shut your computer down or close the notepad window without saving your work first, your wonderful grocery list will be lost forever.

Opening Notepad: Visual Instructions

Step One:
Place your mouse arrow on the START button. Click one time.

Step Two:
Place your mouse on the option ALL PROGRAMS.

Step Three:
Slide your mouse pointer into the Programs submenu. Find and highlight ACCESSORIES.

Step Four:
Slide into the Accessories menu. Click on the NOTEPAD option.

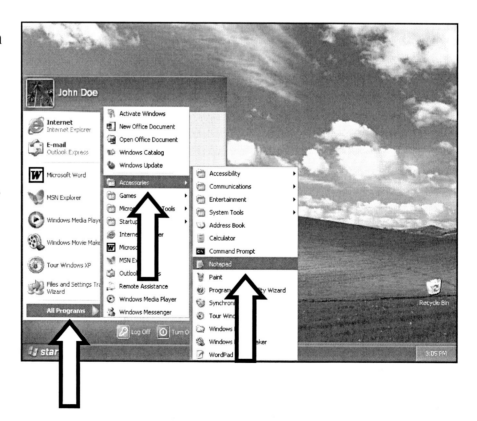

Locate your blinking cursor.

Note that your title bar says "UNTITLED."

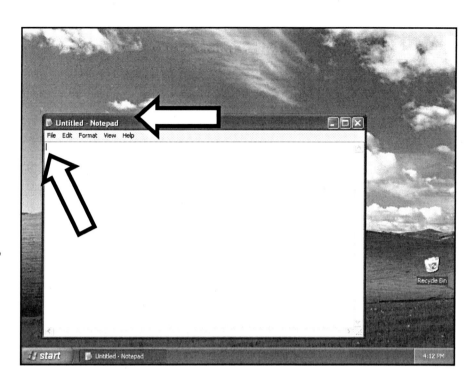

Type:
Milk

Press:
ENTER key

Type:
Eggs

Press:
ENTER key

Type:
Cheese

Chapter 7: Saving Your Work

Section 23: Saving to My Documents:
The Grocery List

Saving a Document to the My Documents Folder:

Note: Your title bar is labeled "Untitled". Your title bar will change after you save your work.

1. Click on the FILE menu located in the upper left hand corner of the window
2. Click on the option SAVE
3. The "Save As" screen will appear
    *   The "Save As" screen enables you to save your work to your computer
    *   In order to save your work to the computer, you have to tell the computer two things: where you want to save your work and what you want to name your new file.
4. Tell the computer where you want to save your work first. Look in the upper left hand corner of the "Save As" screen. You will see the words "Save In:" and directly to the right of those words will be a drop down box. The computer will save your work to whatever *location* is written in this drop down box. You can change the contents of this drop down box by clicking on the drop down arrow. The drop down arrow is the triangular blue arrow found at the end of the box. Clicking the drop down arrow will display a list of the locations on your computer in which you can save your work.
5. You want to choose the option "My Documents".
    *   Place your mouse pointer on the option "My Documents" from the list and click your left mouse button once. The name will move to the Save In: box.

- You have just successfully told the computer that you want to save your work in the "My Documents" folder.

6. Now you have to give your new file a name. Near the bottom of the "Save As" screen are the words FILE NAME. Directly to the right of this box is a white input box where you can type the name of your new file. Giving your new file a name will help you find it later.

7. Click in the file name box one time with the left mouse button. Any text inside the file name input box will turn blue. Press either the Delete key or the Backspace key to erase anything in the input box.

8. Once everything has been erased from the input box, simply type a descriptive name for your new file. In this example, the name "Grocery list" would make the most sense.

9. Once you have chosen a location, My Documents, and a name, grocery list, you are ready to click the "Save" button. The SAVE button is in the lower right hand corner of the "Save As" screen. Place your mouse pointer over the SAVE button and click one time with your left mouse button.

10. Congratulations, your grocery list has been saved!

Saving a Document to the My Documents Folder: Visual Guide

Step One:
Click on the
FILE menu.

Step Two:
Click the
SAVE option.

The top drop down box needs to read "My Documents"

Step Three: Click on the down arrow to see a list of all of the drawers on our computer.

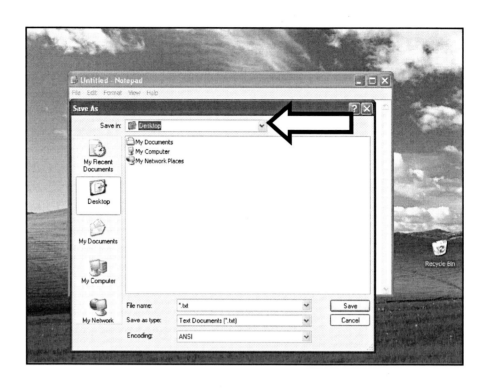

Step Four: Click the MY DOCUMENTS option from the list.

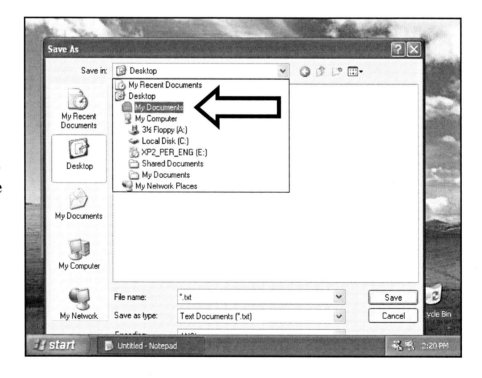

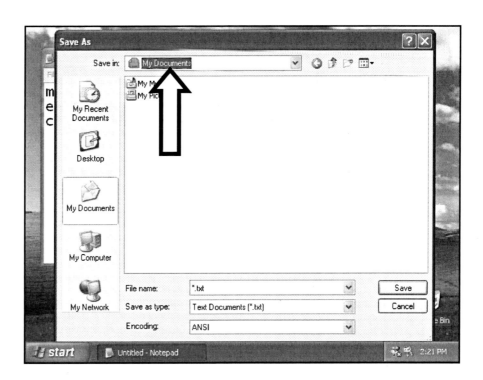

"My Documents" will appear in the top drop down box.

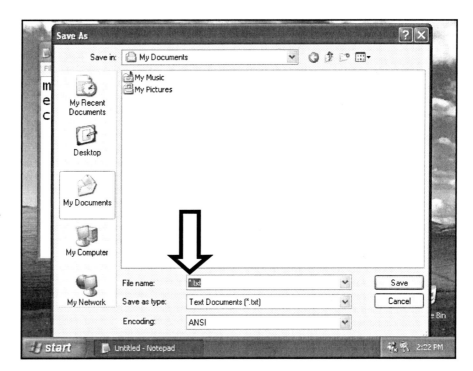

Step Five:
Click in the FILE NAME input box one time.

The text currently in the box will turn blue.

149

Step Six:
Use the
BACKSPACE
or DELETE
key to erase the
contents of the
box.

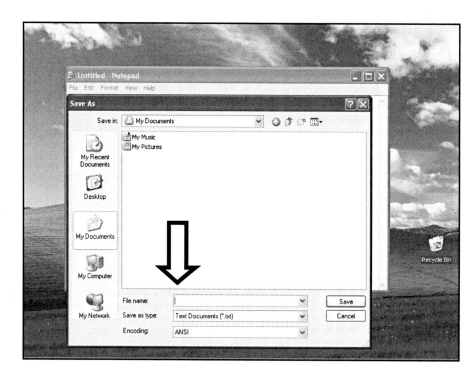

Step Seven:
Type a new
name for your
new document.

In this
example, type
"Grocery List"

Step Eight:
Click the
SAVE button.

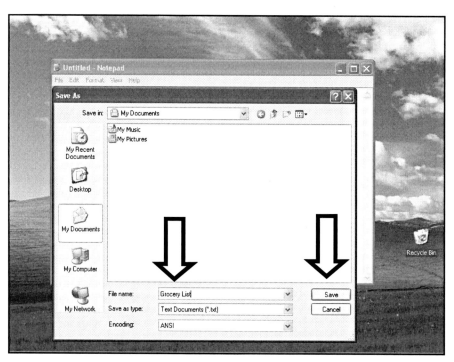

After clicking the SAVE button, you should automatically be returned to your grocery list. Take a look at the title bar of your grocery list window. It is no longer labeled "Untitled". It will display the name of your document. In this case, it should say Grocery List.

Your work has been saved to your computer's My Documents folder.

NOTE: Look at your title bar. In this example, it should say Grocery List.

Click the "X" to close the Grocery List.

Closing the Grocery List window will allow us to practice finding it on your computer.

Chapter 7: Saving Your Work

Section 24: Finding a Document Saved to the My Documents Folder

Finding Items Saved in the My Documents Folder: Step by Step Instructions

Click the "X" in the upper right hand corner of your grocery list to close the window. You should be back to your desktop. Make sure there are no programs open on the computer screen. Now, you know you saved your grocery list. So where is it? To find where you stored your grocery list you need to look in your Start menu.

1. **Click on the START button.**
2. **Move your mouse arrow up to the option MY DOCUMENTS.**
3. **Click on the option MY DOCUMENTS**
   - **A window will appear displaying the contents of the "My Documents" folder.**
   - **One of the items contained in the "My Documents" window will be your grocery list.**
4. **Place your mouse arrow above the grocery list icon and double click.**
   - **The grocery list will re-open.**

Hint: If you have trouble double clicking to open icons there is an alternative. Click once on the icon and the icon will turn blue or in technical terms the icon will become highlighted. Once the icon has been highlighted, press the ENTER key on the keyboard and the icon will open.

Remember: When you click on an icon, always click on the picture, not the name. Clicking on the picture ensures that the computer knows what to do.

Chapter 7: Saving Your Work

Finding Items Saved in the My Documents Folder: Visual Guide

Step One: Place your mouse arrow on the START button and click one time.

The START menu will open.

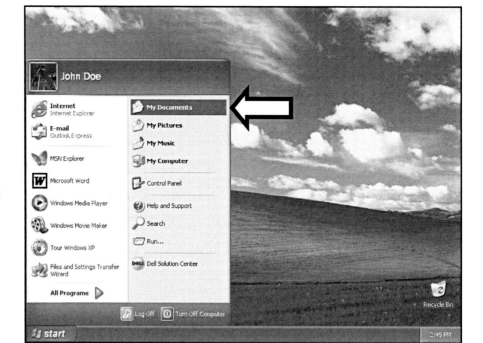

**Step Two:
Click on the
option MY
DOCUMENTS**

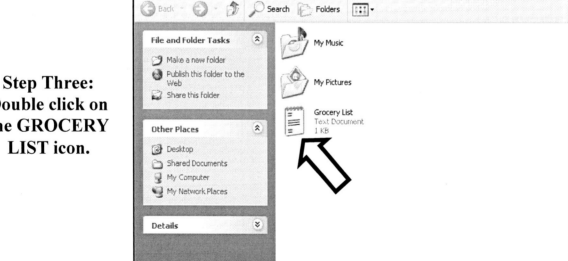

**Step Three:
Double click on
the GROCERY
LIST icon.**

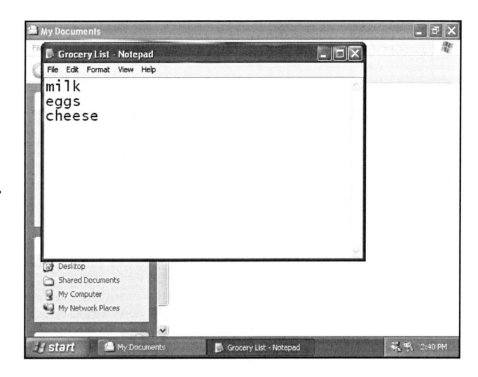

The GROCERY LIST will open.

Section 25: Save vs. Save As

Question: What is the difference between Save and Save As?

Answer: Great question! First, click once on the FILE menu of your grocery list. Remember, the File Menu is located in the upper left corner of your Notepad window. Once the menu has opened, take a look at the listed options. You will see the SAVE option, but just below it is the SAVE AS option. There is no difference between the two options the *first time* you save an item. Both options will bring up the same "Save As" screen. Yes, you understood that correctly. When you save *a brand new document*, it does not matter whether you choose SAVE or SAVE AS. They will both do the same thing. The two options differ when working with existing documents. By definition, SAVE will save any changes you make to a document *to the original document*. For example, if you added ham and cookies to your grocery list and clicked on the SAVE option you would end up with one file named "Grocery List" that contained the items milk, eggs, cheese, ham, and cookies.

By definition, SAVE AS gives you the opportunity to save your changes to a different copy of your document leaving the original document unchanged. Every time you choose SAVE AS, the Save As: screen appears providing you with the opportunity to choose either a new location for your changes, a new name, or both. If you change either the name or the location in the Save As screen, you will end up with two copies of your work, your original and your changed version. For example. If you add ham and cookies to your grocery list and choose Save As, the save as screen will appear. You can change the file name to "Grocery List 2." You will now have two grocery lists. One with milk, eggs, and cheese named "Grocery List" and one list with eggs, milk, cheese, ham, and cookies named "Grocery List 2."

REMINDER:
Save: saves any changes you make to a document to the original document.

Save As: gives you the opportunity to save your changes to a copy of your document leaving the original document unchanged.

To further explain and illustrate these ideas let's walk through these steps together.

If you are following along, you will have your grocery list open on your desktop. So far, your grocery list contains milk, eggs, and cheese. Add ham and cookies to the list.

Saving Additional Changes using the SAVE Option: Visual Instructions

Click after the word CHEESE.

Press the ENTER key

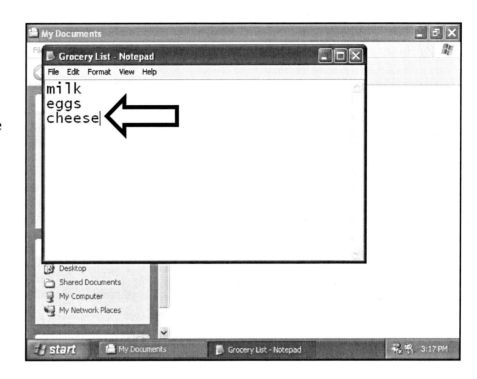

Type the word HAM.

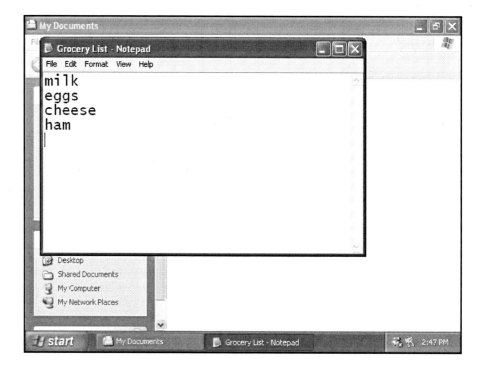

**Press the
ENTER key.**

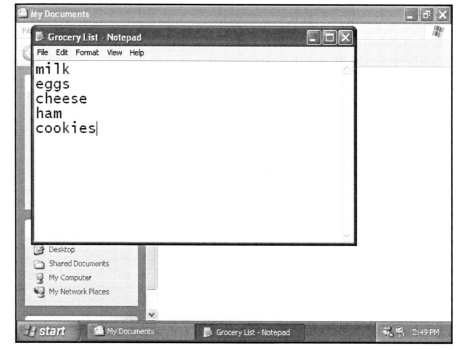

**Type the word
COOKIES.**

Click on your FILE menu and choose the option SAVE by clicking on it one time with your left mouse button. After you click on the option Save, it will seem like nothing happened but, trust me, your work has been saved. You do not need to go through a SAVE AS screen because the computer already knows where this document is located and what the document is named. It is named "Grocery List" and it is located in the My Documents folder. You chose the name "Grocery List" and the location My Documents the first time you saved the list. When you clicked on SAVE the computer simply saved the additions, ham and cookies, to your original list. You now still have only one list including the items milk, eggs, cheese, ham, and cookies.

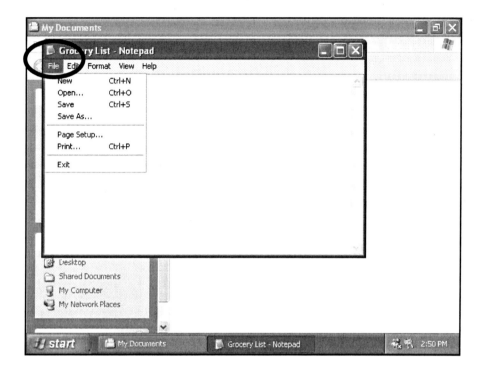

Click on the FILE menu

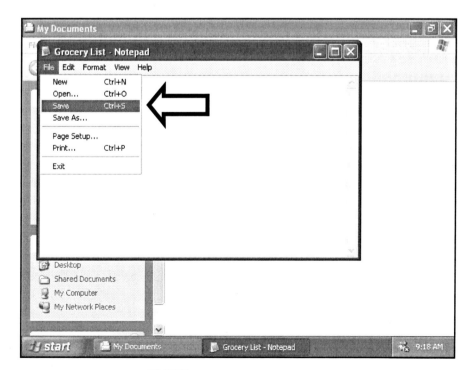

Click on the option SAVE.

Your changes have been recorded.

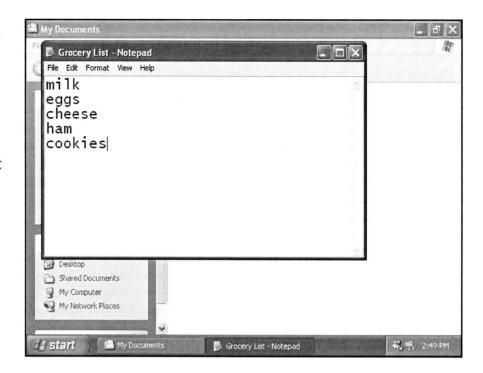

You now have one grocery list including ham and cookies.

Now, add beans to the list.

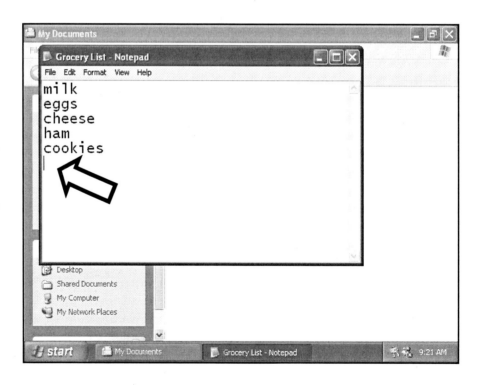

Press the ENTER key on the keyboard to move the blinking cursor down one line.

Add BEANS to the list.

Saving Changes Using the SAVE AS Option: Step by Step Instructions

In this example, you will use the SAVE AS option.

1. **Click on the FILE menu and choose SAVE AS by clicking on it with your left mouse button.**
   - **This time the Save As screen appears.**
2. **Click in the FILE NAME box.**
   - **Using the Backspace key and/or the Delete key erase any contents of the file name box.**
3. **Type in the new name of Grocery List 2.**
4. **Click the SAVE button in the bottom right corner of the Save As screen.**

You now have two grocery lists. Both are saved in My Documents but they have different names. One list has beans and the second does not have beans. Go to the My Documents folder to see this for yourself. Click the "X" in the upper right corner of the Grocery List 2 window. This will close the window. Now look at the My Documents window. (You will know you are looking in the My Documents window because it says My Documents in the window's title bar.) You will see grocery list and grocery list 2 in the My Documents window. Double click on both files. This will open the lists and allow you to see the differences for yourself.

Chapter 7: Saving Your Work

Saving Changes Using the SAVE AS Option: Visual Guide

**Step One:
Click on the
FILE menu.**

**Step Two:
Click the
SAVE AS
option.**

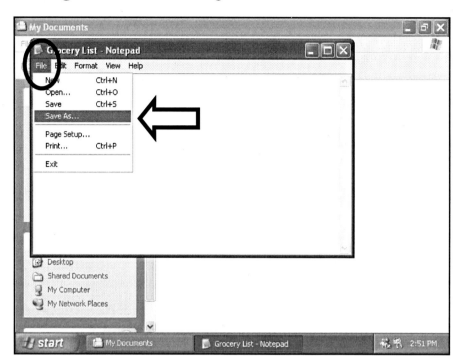

**Step Three:
Press the
BACKSPACE
key to erase the
name of the
original
grocery list.**

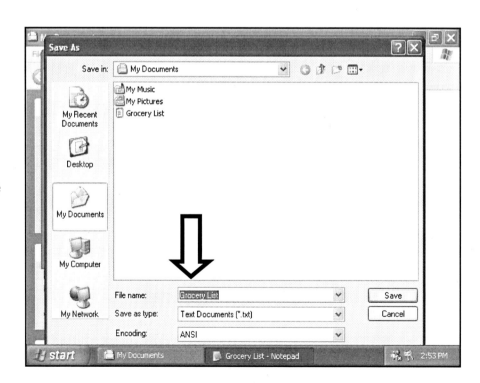

Step Four:
Type a new name for your new grocery list.

In this example, type in "Grocery List 2"

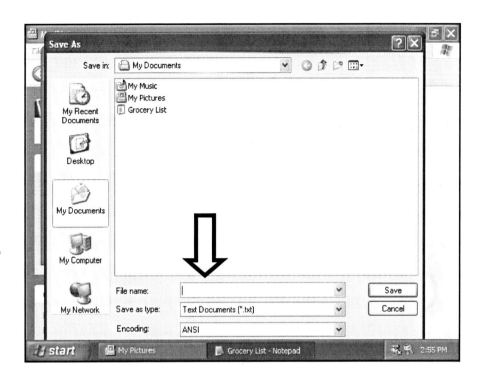

Step Five:
Click on the SAVE button.

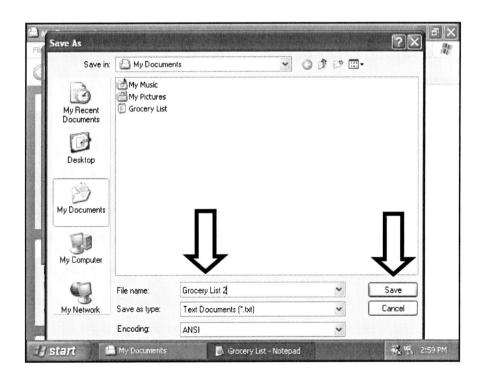

Step Six:
Click the Close (X) button.

Both grocery lists have been saved in the My Documents folder.

List 2 has beans, the other list doesn't.

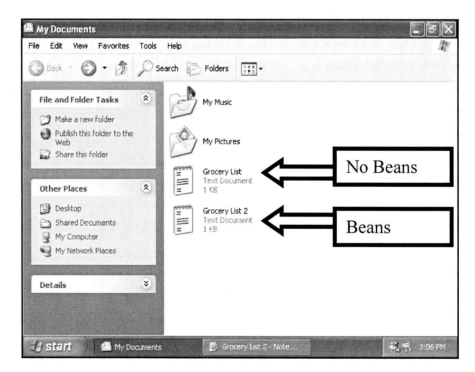

Section 26: Saving a document to a floppy disk

Introduction

Saving a document to a floppy disk is very similar to saving a document to the "My Documents" folder. There are only a couple steps that differ. To practice, create a recipe and save the recipe to a floppy disk. Step one is to open your word processing program so you can create your recipe.

Opening Notepad: Step by Step Instructions

1. Click on the START BUTTON
2. Highlight the option ALL PROGRAMS
3. Highlight the option ACCESSORIES
4. Highlight the option NOTEPAD
5. Click on the option NOTEPAD

Open the
program
NOTEPAD

Chapter 7: Saving Your Work

Creating a Document to Save to the Floppy Disk

After you open notepad you should see the blinking cursor in the upper left hand corner of the notepad window. If the blinking cursor is not there, take your mouse arrow and click anywhere inside the notepad window. The blinking cursor will appear. After you have located your blinking cursor you can begin typing your recipe. In this example you will type up a simple recipe for meatloaf.

Creating the Meatloaf Recipe

1. Type: Grandma's Famous Meatloaf Recipe
2. Press the Enter key twice to move the blinking cursor down two lines.
3. Type: Combine seasoning with 2 lbs. of ground beef, 2 eggs, 1/2 cup milk, and 2 slices of bread crumbs.
4. Press the Enter key twice to move the blinking cursor down two lines
5. Type: Shape into a loaf in a shallow baking pan.
6. Press the Enter key twice to move the blinking cursor down two lines
7. Type: Preheat oven to 375 degrees.
8. Press the Enter key twice to move the blinking cursor down two lines
9. Type: Bake 1 hour.

Creating a Document: Visual Instructions

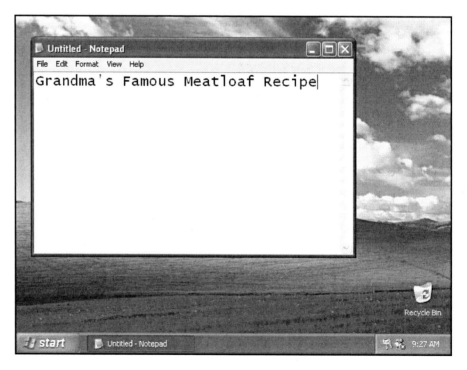

Step One:
Add title

Step Two: Press the ENTER key twice.

Step Three: Type the ingredients.

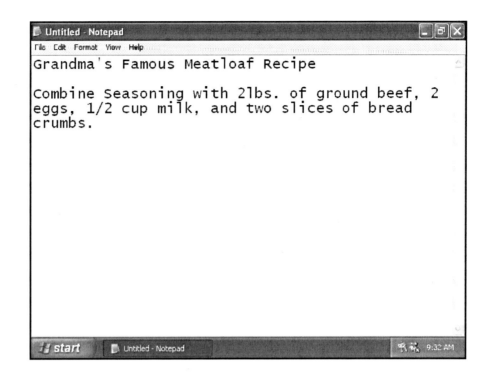

Step Four: Press the ENTER key twice.

Step Five: Type the directions.

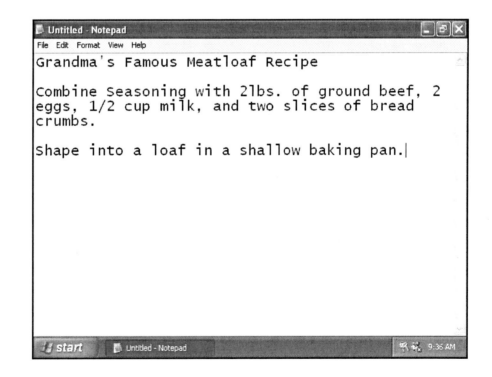

Step Six:
Press the
ENTER key
twice.

Step Seven:
Type the
directions.

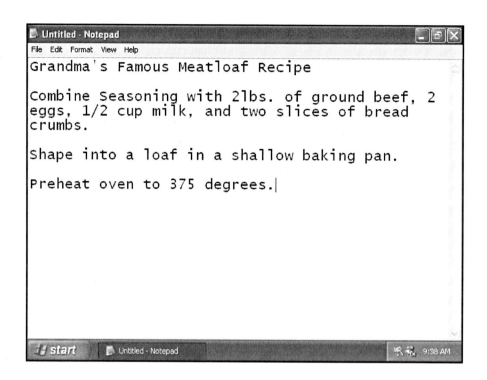

Step Eight:
Press the
ENTER key
twice.

Step Nine:
Type the last
line of
directions.

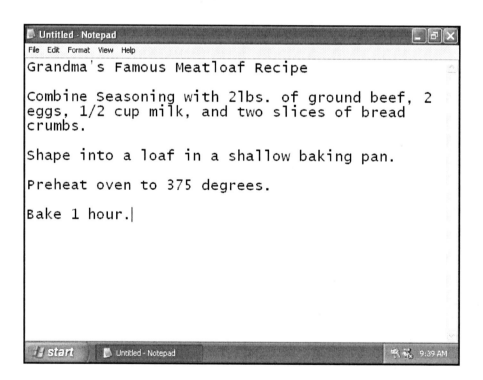

Chapter 7: Saving Your Work

***Saving your work to a Floppy Disk:* Step by Step Instructions**

Now that your recipe has been completed you need to save your work. This time you will save your work to a floppy disk.

1. Insert a floppy disk into the floppy disk drive
   - Note that your title bar is labeled "Untitled." Your title bar will change after you save your work.
2. Click on the FILE menu located in the upper left hand corner of the window.
3. Click on the option SAVE.
4. The "Save As" screen will appear
   - The "Save As" screen enables you to save your work to your computer.
   - In order to save your work to the computer you have to tell the computer two things: where you want to save your work and what you want to name your new file. The "Save As" screen enables you to accomplish this.
   - Tell the computer where you want to save your work first. Look in the upper left hand corner of the "Save As" screen. You will see the words "Save In:" and directly to the right of those words will be a drop down box. The computer will save your work to whatever location is written in this drop down box. You can change the contents of this drop down box by clicking on the drop down arrow. The drop down arrow is the triangular blue arrow found at the end of the box. Clicking the drop down arrow will display a list of the locations on your computer in which you can save your work.
   - You want to choose the option "3 1/2 floppy (A:)".
5. Click on the option "3 1/2 floppy (A:)" from the list. It will jump to the top box.
   - You have just successfully told the computer that you want to save your work in the "3 1/2 floppy (A:)".
6. Now, you have to give your new file a name. Near the bottom of the "Save As" screen are the words FILE NAME. Directly to the right of this box is a white input box where you can type the name of your new file. Giving your new file a name will help you find it later. Press either the Delete key or the Backspace key to erase anything in the input box.

169

7. Once everything has been erased from the input box, type a descriptive name for your new file. In this example, the name "Meatloaf Recipe" would make the most sense.

8. After you have chosen a location, 3 1/2 floppy (A:), and a name, Meatloaf Recipe, you are ready to click the SAVE button in the lower right hand corner of the "Save As" screen. Congratulations, your grocery list has been saved to your floppy disk!

Saving your work to a floppy disk: Visual Guide

Step One:
Place a floppy disk into the floppy disk drive

Step Two
Click on the FILE menu.

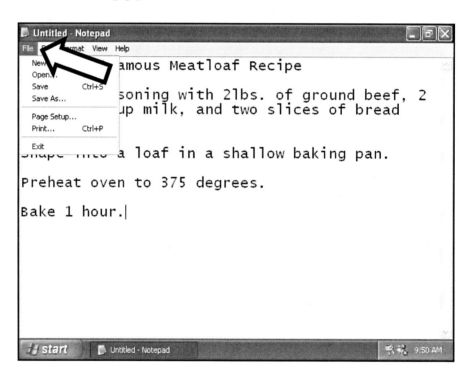

Chapter 7: Saving Your Work

Step Three:
Click the
SAVE option.

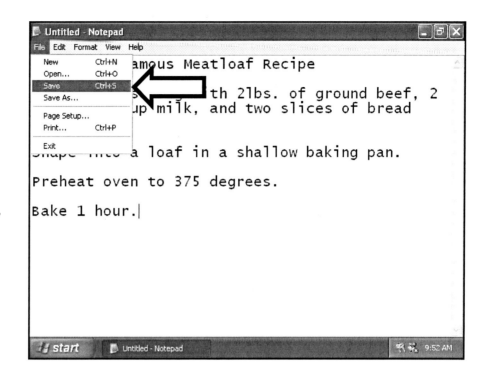

Step Four:
Click on the
drop down
arrow.

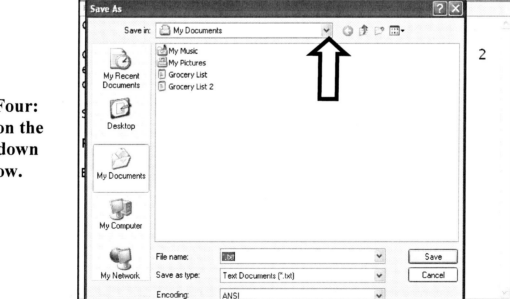

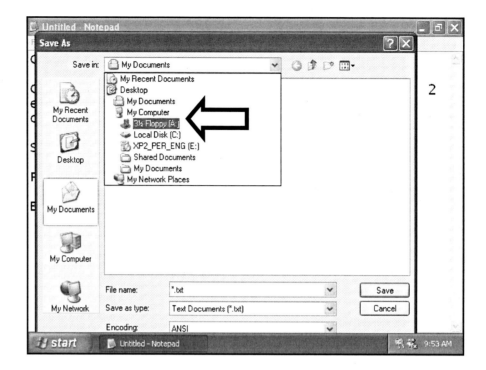

**Step Five:
Click on the
option 3 ½
Floppy (A:).**

**3 ½ Floppy
(A:) will jump
to the Save In:
box."**

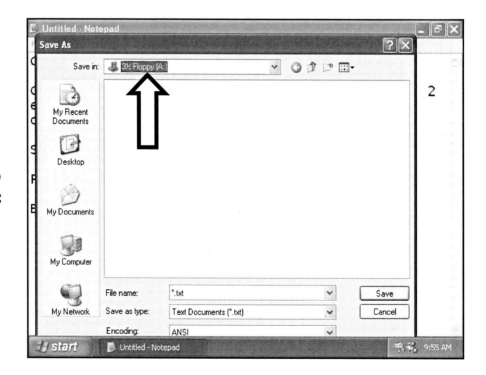

CAUTION:
If you forget to insert a floppy disk you will receive the following message.

Insert a floppy disk and the message will go away.

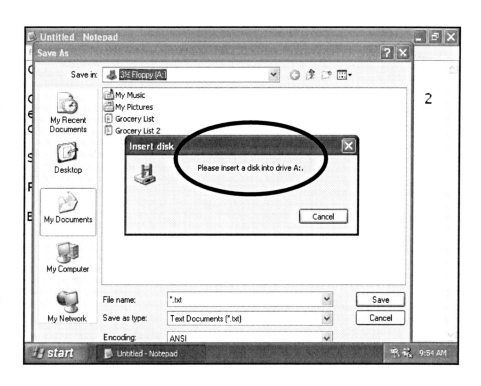

Step Six:
Click in the FILE NAME box one time.

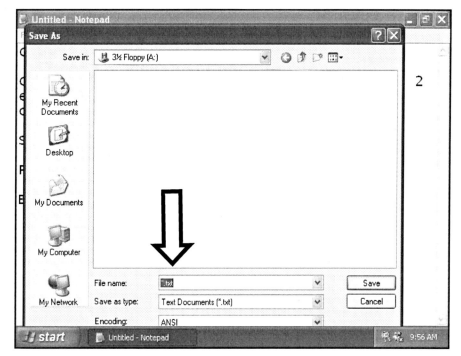

Step Seven: Press the BACKSPACE key on the keyboard to erase the current file name.

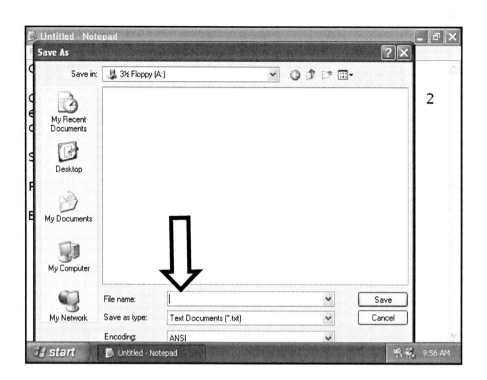

Step Eight: Type in the new file name.

In this example, type "Meatloaf Recipe"

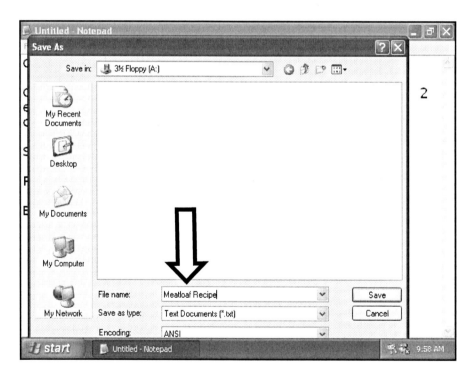

After clicking the "Save" button, you should automatically be returned to your meatloaf recipe. Take a look at the title bar of your meatloaf recipe window. It is no longer labeled "Untitled". It will display the name of your document. In this case, it should say "Meatloaf Recipe."

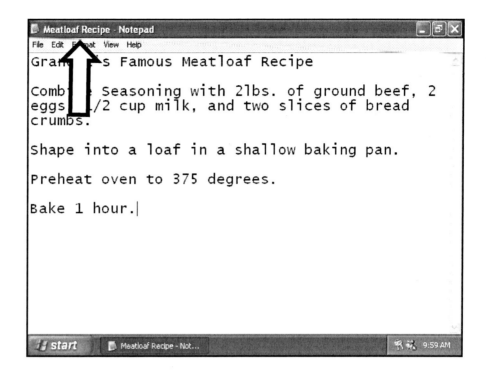

The title bar now reads "Meatloaf Recipe"

Click the "X" in the upper right hand corner of your meatloaf recipe to close the window. You should end up back at your desktop screen.

Chapter 7: Saving Your Work

Section 27: Accessing Information Stored on a Floppy Disk

Accessing Information on a Floppy Disk

Now, you want to find your meatloaf recipe. To find where you stored your meatloaf recipe you need to look in your Start menu.

1. Make sure the floppy disk you saved your work to is in the floppy disk drive.
2. Click on the START button.
3. Move your mouse arrow up to the option MY COMPUTER.
4. Click on the option MY COMPUTER.
5. A window will appear displaying the contents of "My Computer". One of the items contained in the "My Computer" window will be your 3 1/2 floppy (A:) drive. If you don't see the 3 1/2 floppy (A:) drive, use your scroll bar to move down the screen to bring the floppy drive into view. Place your mouse arrow above the 3 1/2 floppy (A:) icon and double click. If you double click successfully, the contents of your floppy disk will be displayed. Another way to know you double clicked successfully is to look in the title bar of your window. It should say 3 1/2 floppy (A:). One of the items in the 3 1/2 floppy (A:) window will be your meatloaf recipe.
6. Place your mouse arrow above the meatloaf recipe icon and double click. The meatloaf recipe will re-open.

Hint: All floppy disks come with a set of labels. Place these labels on your floppy disks and use them. Having to sort through unlabeled floppy disks to find where you stored something can be a nightmare.

Accessing Information Stored on a Floppy Disk: Visual

Step One:
Click on the
START menu.

Step Two:
Click on the
option
MY
COMPUTER.

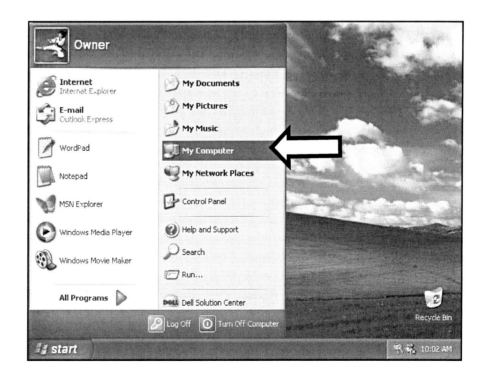

177

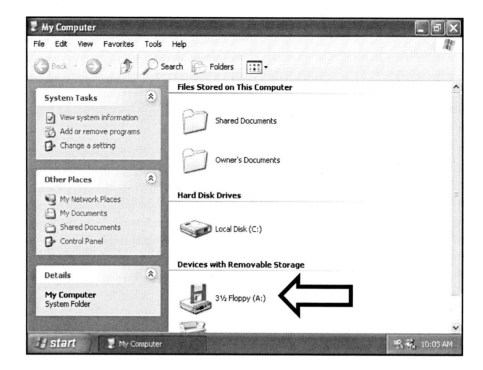

Step Three: Click on the option 3 ½ Floppy (A:).

Step Four: Double click the meatloaf recipe.

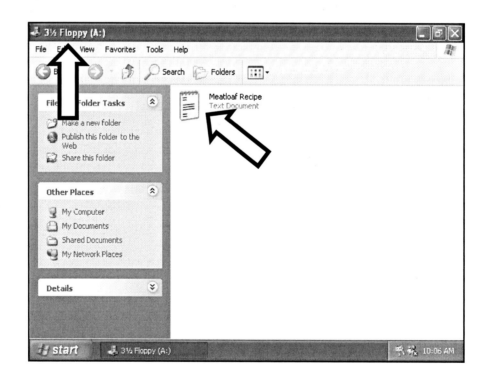

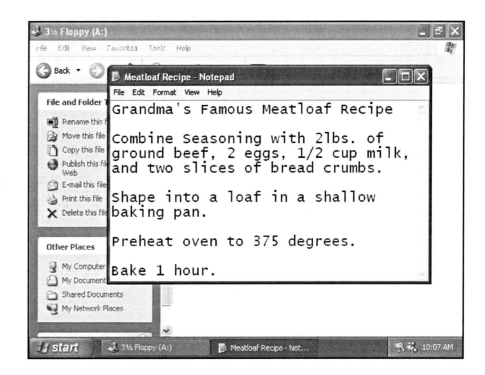

A successful double click will open your meatloaf recipe.

Section 28: Backing up Files

What Does the Term Backing Up Mean?

Computer users often use the term "backing up." Backing up your computer files means saving your files to more than one location so, if one copy is accidentally erased or ruined, you have a second copy to work from. Floppy disks are commonly used to back up computer files. People save their work to the "My Documents" folder as well as to a floppy disk. To "back up" your important files, the first step is to open the file on your computer. If you have been following along, open up the grocery list that you saved earlier in the "My

Documents" folder. After you have opened your file, follow the same steps to save your work as you always do.

Backing up an Important File to a Floppy Disk: **Step by Step Instructions**

1. Open the file you want to back up. In this example, "Grocery List."
2. Click on the FILE menu and choose the option SAVE AS.
    - The "Save As" screen will appear. The "Save As" screen enables you to save your work.
    - ***REMINDER:*** In order to save your work to the computer you have to tell the computer two things: where you want to save your work and what you want to name your new file. The "Save As" screen enables you to accomplish this.
3. Tell the computer where you want to save your work first. Take a look in the upper left hand corner of the "Save As" screen. You will see the words "Save In" and directly to the right of those words will be a drop down box. This drop down box tells you where the computer is going to save your work. You can change the contents of this drop down box by clicking on the drop down arrow. This will display a list of all the places on your computer in which you can save your work.
4. You want to choose the option "3 1/2 floppy (A:)." Choose the option "3 1/2 floppy (A:)" from the list by clicking on it with your left mouse button. It will jump to the box at the top of the window. You have just successfully told the computer that you want to save your work in the "3 1/2 floppy (A:)".
5. Now you have to give your file a name. Near the bottom of the "Save As" screen are the words "File Name". Directly to the right of this box is a white input box where you can name your new file. Since this file has already been saved to the My Documents folder, the name "Grocery List" should already appear in the box. If you want to change the name, you can do so, but, since we are only backing up the file, there is no real need to change it.
6. After you have chosen a location, 3 1/2 floppy (A:), and a name, "Grocery List" you are ready to click the SAVE button in the lower right hand corner of the "Save As" screen. Congratulations, you have successfully backed up your grocery list to a floppy disk! Now if you lose your original grocery list stored on your computer you will always have a second copy on your floppy disk.

Chapter 7: Saving Your Work

Backing up an Important File to a Floppy Disk: Visual Guide

Step One:
Locate the file you want to backup.

Step Two:
Double click the file to open it.

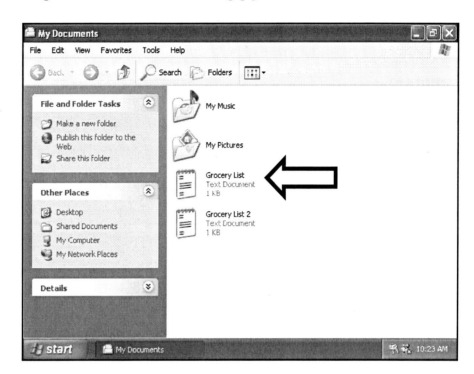

Step Three:
Click on the FILE Menu.

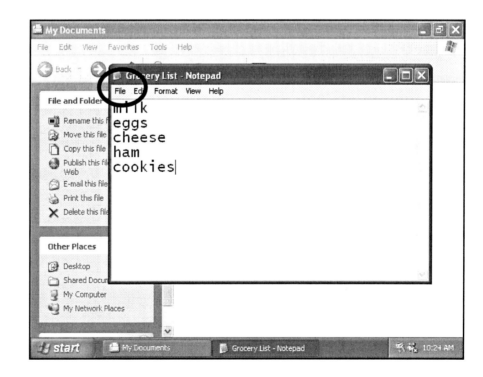

Step Four: Click the SAVE AS option.

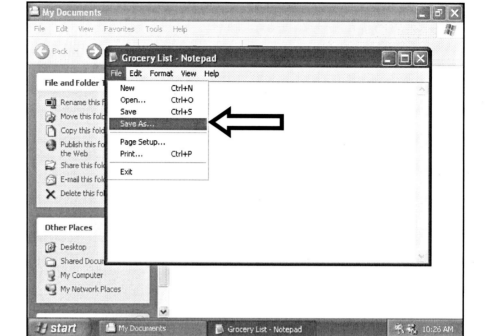

Step Five: Click on the drop down arrow.

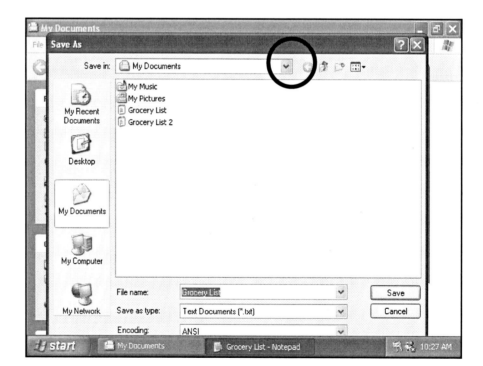

Step Six:
Click on the
option 3 ½
Floppy (A:).

Step Seven:
If you want to
change the
file's name,
you can, but it
is not
necessary.

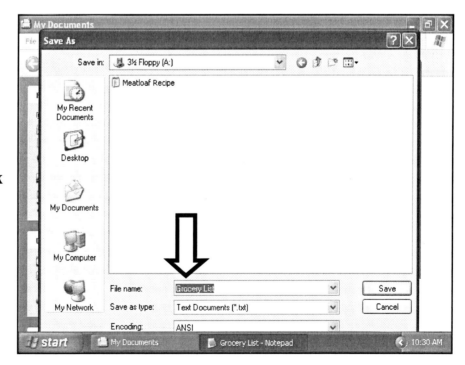

**Step Eight:
Click the
SAVE Button**

**You have
successfully
backed up your
grocery list to a
floppy disk.**

Chapter 8

Organizing Your Computer

What You Will Learn in This Chapter
- ✓ How to create a new folder.
- ✓ How to rename a folder.
- ✓ How to move files & folders around on your computer.

Section 29: Creating Folders

Introduction

So far, you have learned that you can store your work on floppy disks and on the computer in the "My Documents" folder. These are two great storage places but, after working with your computer for a time, they will eventually become cluttered. Imagine having a refrigerator with only one drawer. After a while, you would have a difficult time finding anything in the fridge because there would be no easy way to organize it. It is much easier to have a refrigerator with multiple storage places: one drawer for the condiments, one drawer for meats, another one for vegetables, etc. The same principle applies to computers. Assume that you want to store pictures of your vacation, documents for work, and your world famous recipes on your computer. If you store all of them in your "My Documents" folder, you would have one full folder with pictures, documents, and recipes scattered throughout. After a while, it would become difficult to sort through all of these items. To avoid this dilemma, you need to learn to organize your "My Documents" folder. You can organize your "My Documents" folder by creating subfolders inside the "My Documents" folder. This way each item that you save to your computer can have its very own folder to be categorized within. How you organize your computer is up to you. You can create as few or as many folders as you like.

Creating a New Folder: **Step by Step Instructions**

1. The first step in creating a new folder is to go to the location where you want to create the folder. In this example you will be creating a new folder in "My Documents" so go to "My Documents." If your my documents folder is not already open, click on the START button to open up the Start Menu. Move your mouse arrow up to the option MY DOCUMENTS and click once. The "My Documents" window will open. Now that you have chosen a location, you are ready to create the new folder.

2. Move your mouse arrow over the FILE menu located in the upper right hand corner of the "My Documents" window and click once with your left mouse button to open the file menu.

3. The top option that appears in the File menu will be NEW. Slide your mouse arrow down to NEW.

4. You will notice a small black arrow to the right of the word NEW. This arrow lets you know that there is more to this option. When you place your mouse pointer over the NEW option, a submenu will appear to the right of NEW. Slide your mouse arrow directly to the right, staying within the blue highlight until your mouse arrow is in the submenu.

5. The top option in the submenu will be FOLDER. Place your mouse arrow above the option FOLDER and click the left mouse button ONE time. A new folder will appear in your "My Documents" window.

Warning: Do NOT click anymore! If you click again you will lose the opportunity to change the name of your new folder and the newly created folder will be given the unhelpful name of "New Folder." Take your hand off the mouse once your new folder has been created.

6. Take a look at the new folder you created. You should have a picture (icon) of a yellow folder and next to the folder will be the words "New Folder" highlighted in blue. Remember, the blue highlight tells you what the computer is currently looking at and what the computer is ready to work with. You do not want to keep the name "New Folder" for your new folder. You want to give it a more descriptive name.

7. To change the folders name, press the "Backspace" key on your keyboard to erase the highlighted name "New folder". The folder's name should be erased and you should be left with a blinking cursor in the box.

8. Type a name for the new folder. In this example, name the folder Recipes.

9. Once you have given the folder a new name, you need to tell the computer you are done. (Until you tell the computer you are done, the blinking cursor will flash in the name box waiting for you to continue adding to or changing the folder's name.) To tell the computer you are ready to move on, move your mouse arrow to any white portion of your "My Documents" window and click the left mouse button one

time. You have just created a new folder named recipes where you can store all of your world famous creations!

Creating a New Folder: Visual Guide

**Step One:
Go to your
MY
DOCUMENTS
folder.**

**Step Two:
Click on the
FILE Menu.**

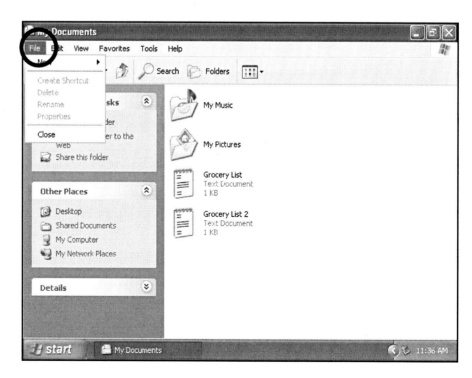

Step Three: Highlight the option NEW.

Step Four: A submenu will appear. Slide the mouse arrow into the NEW submenu.

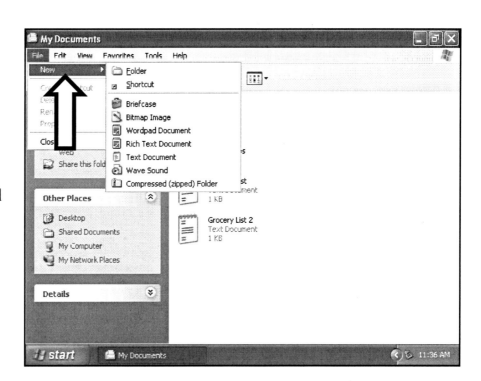

Step Five: Highlight the option FOLDER and click ONE time.

WARNING: Do NOT click again!

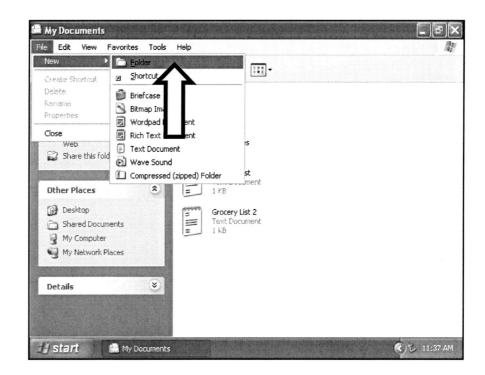

Step Six:
Press the
BACKSPACE
key on the
keyboard to
erase the new
folder's
current name.

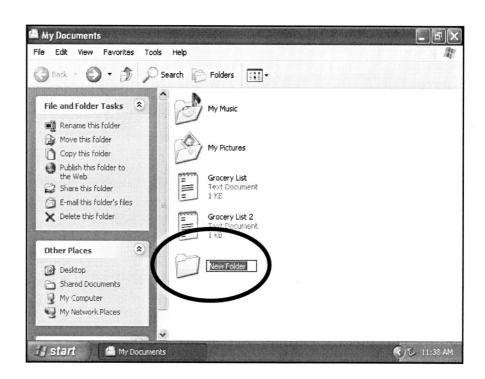

Step Seven:
Type the new
name of the
folder.

In this example
type:
RECIPES

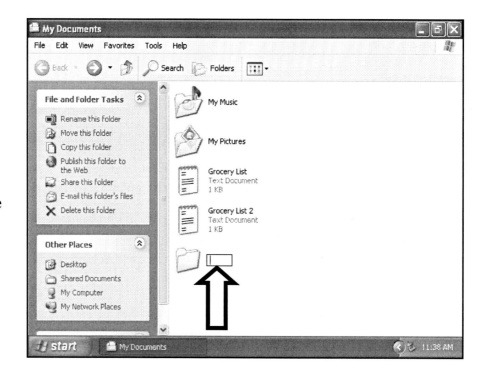

Step Eight: Click the mouse arrow anywhere in the white area of the screen.

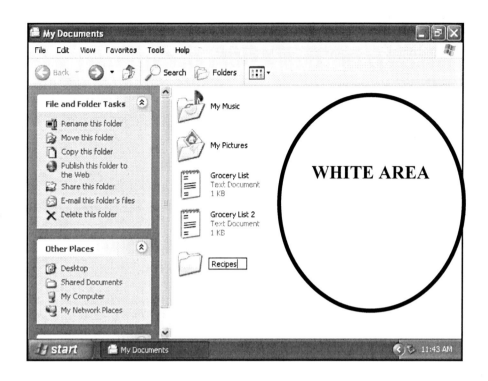

A new folder has been created.

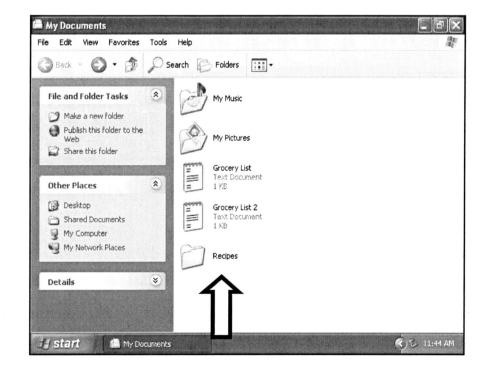

Chapter 8: Organizing Your Computer

Section 30: Renaming a File or Folder

Renaming a Folder: Step by Step Instructions

What would happen if you clicked too many when creating a folder or if you misspelled the name of the folder? Well, first, do not worry; it is not a world ending error. In either case, you do have the ability to change the name of the folder. In this example you will change the name of the recipes folder you created in the previous section.

1. The first step in changing the name of the folder is to tell the computer which folder you want to rename. You do this by clicking on the folder one time. This will highlight the folder in blue. Remember, once something is blue, it means the computer is focused on it.

2. Once the folder you want to rename is highlighted in blue, you need to move your mouse arrow onto the FILE menu located in the upper left hand corner of the window. Click the left mouse button one time and the FILE menu will open.

3. Slide your mouse arrow down the file menu until the arrow is on top of the option RENAME. Click the left mouse button one time on the option RENAME. Do NOT click anymore! Take your hand off the mouse. Take a look at your folder. The folder is no longer highlighted in blue. The computer has changed its focus to the name of the folder. You can tell this has happened because only the name of the folder is now blue.

4. Your next step is to press the Backspace button on the keyboard. The backspace button will erase the folder's previous name.

5. Type a new name. In this example, type the name "Grocery Lists." After you type in the name of your new folder you need to tell the computer that you are done. To do so, move your mouse arrow anywhere in the white area of your "My Documents" window and click the left mouse button one time. The folder has been renamed.

Renaming a Folder: Visual Guide

Step One:
Click one time
on the desired
folder/file.

It will become
highlighted.

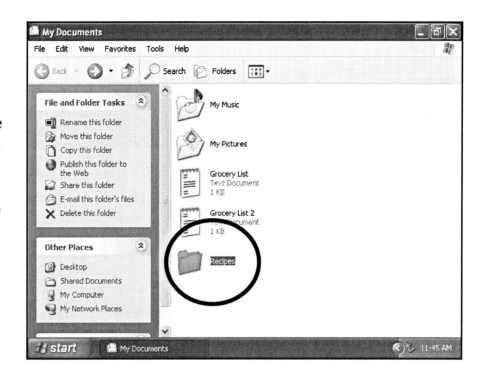

Step Two:
Click on the
FILE Menu.

Step Three:
Click on the
option
RENAME.

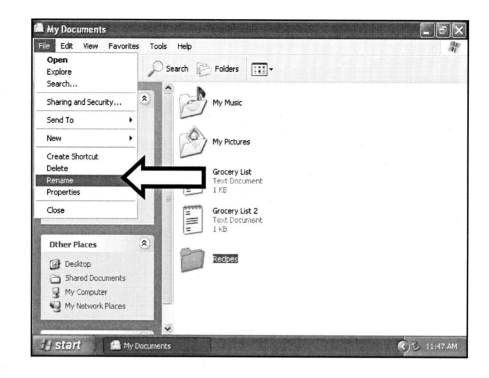

Step Four:
Press the
BACKSPACE
key on the
keyboard.

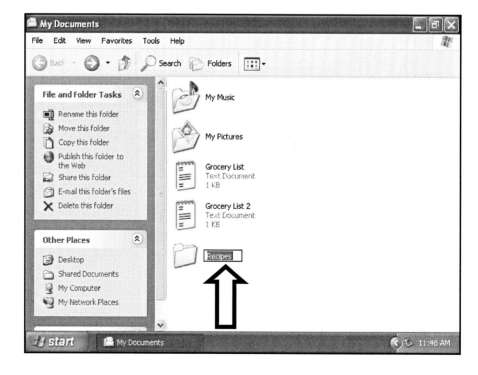

**Step Five:
Type the new
name.**

**In this
example, type:
GROCERY
LISTS.**

**Step Six:
Click the
mouse arrow
anywhere in
the white area
of the screen.**

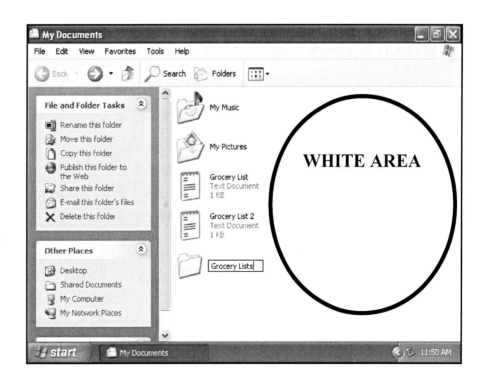

You have renamed the folder/file.

Section 31: Moving Items Stored on Your Computer

Reorganizing your Computer: Step by Step Instructions

Once you have created folders and have saved documents to your computer, you can always return to those items and change their location within the computer. You can change the location of the items on your computer by "clicking and dragging." You used "clicking and dragging" in Solitaire to move the cards around the screen. To demonstrate how to move items around your computer you should look inside "My Documents." You have already created and saved two documents (Grocery List & Grocery List 2) to "My

Documents". You have also created a folder named Grocery Lists. The problem is that all three items are in the "My Documents" folder. It would make more sense if the grocery lists were actually inside the Grocery List folder. Let's move your file Grocery List into the Grocery List folder.

1. Take your mouse arrow and place it above the "Grocery List" document.
2. Click your left mouse button and hold the button down. As long as you hold down the left mouse button, the grocery list document will follow your mouse arrow wherever you move the arrow.
3. Move the grocery list document on top of the Grocery List folder. If you have the mouse pointer positioned correctly, the folder you desire to place your file into will turn blue. Now, let go of the left mouse button. The grocery list document will disappear from the computer screen. The grocery list document is now located in the Grocery List Folder.

Try the same procedure for the Grocery List 2 document.
1. Place your mouse arrow above the Grocery List 2 document.
2. Press and hold down the left mouse button. As long as you hold down the left mouse button, the document will follow your mouse arrow around the screen.
3. Move the Grocery List 2 document on top of the Grocery List Folder (it will turn blue) and let go of the left mouse button. The grocery list 2 document will also disappear from the screen. It has also been moved inside of the Grocery List folder.

You have just successfully reorganized your computer. Now, in order to view your grocery lists you have to open the Grocery list folder. Place your mouse arrow on top of the grocery list folder and double click your left mouse button. After a successful double click, the contents of the Grocery List folder will be displayed and both grocery lists will be seen inside the window.

REMINDER: Always check your title bar. The title bar will always tell you your location on the computer. When you successfully double click on the Grocery List Folder the title bar will be labeled "Grocery List". When you were looking inside "My Documents" the title bar was labeled "My Documents."

Reorganizing your Computer: Visual Instructions

Step One:
Click on the
file you want to
move and hold
the mouse
button down.

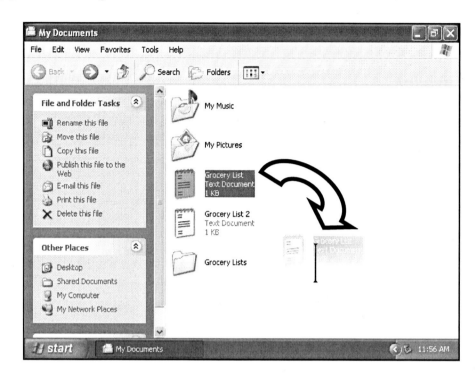

Step Two:
Move your
mouse arrow
on the folder
into which you
want to place
the file.

Step Three:
Let go of the
left mouse
button.

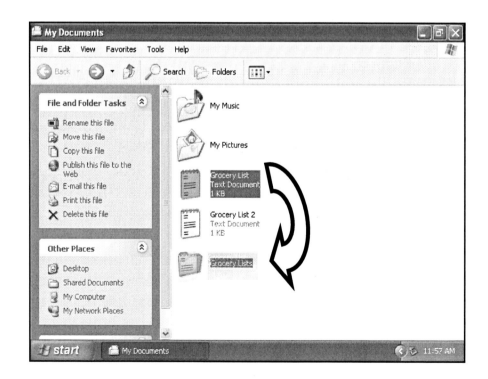

The file is now located inside of the new folder.

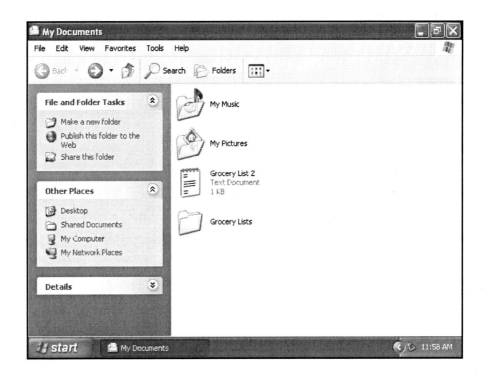

Repeat the same steps with GROCERY LIST 2.

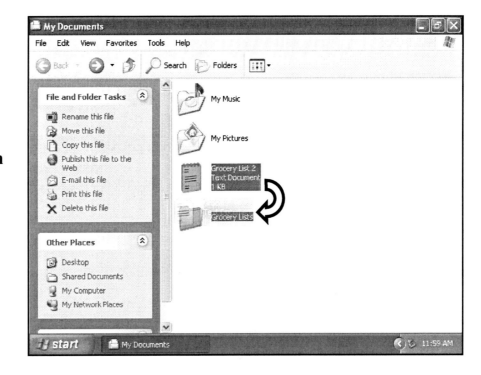

Click on the **GROCERY LIST** folder to view its contents.

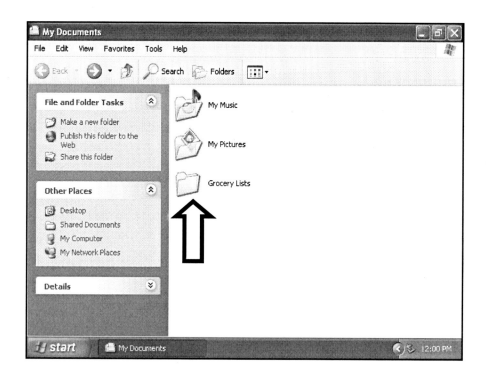

Both grocery lists should now be located inside the **GROCERY LIST** folder.

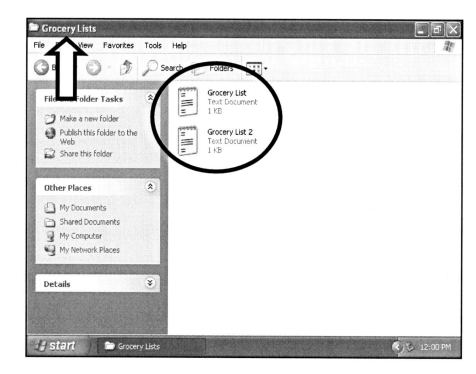

Chapter 9

The Recycle Bin and More

What You Will Learn in This Chapter
- ✓ How to delete files & folders stored on your computer.
- ✓ How to remove deleted files from the recycle bin (aka rescue them).
- ✓ How to empty the recycle bin (aka permanently erase items).
- ✓ How to create shortcuts.
- ✓ How to remove icons from the desktop.
- ✓ Some helpful hints on the concept of highlighting.

Chapter 9: The Recycle Bin & More

Section 32: Deleting Files or Folders

Recycle Bin

The recycle bin functions as a safety valve very much like the garbage can in your kitchen. If you throw away an important piece of information into your kitchen garbage can, you can always go back to it and pull the important piece of information out. If you emptied your kitchen garbage can in Monday's trash pickup, you're out of luck. The same principle applies to your computer's recycle bin. Whenever you delete something from your computer, the deleted item is sent to your recycle bin. As long as you haven't emptied your recycle bin, you can always go back to the bin and retrieve your deleted item. When you retrieve your deleted item, it will be sent back to its original storage place on your computer. For example, if you deleted an item from your My Documents folder, when you retrieve the item from your recycle bin it will reappear back in the My Documents folder.

Deleting Files and Folders: Step by Step Instructions

The process of deletion, throwing items away, is the same for both files and folders. When you delete any file or folder it cleans up your computer. Deleting items helps you get rid of unwanted or old files. It also helps keep the computer running smoothly. Saving something to your computer takes up computer storage space. When this storage space becomes filled, your computer may begin to operate more slowly. It is always a good idea to delete unwanted files and folders.

1. When deleting an item from the computer, you need to first locate the item on your computer. If you have been following along with this book you are inside the Grocery List folder, which holds two items (Grocery List and Grocery List 2).
2. If you want to delete the Grocery List document, place your mouse arrow on the Grocery List document and press the left mouse button one time. The grocery list will become highlighted in blue. Remember, the highlight tells you what the computer is focused on.

3. Now that the grocery list is highlighted in blue, you need to move your mouse arrow up to the FILE menu which is located in the upper left hand corner of the window. Click once on FILE to open the file menu.

4. Move your mouse arrow down the FILE menu list until it is on DELETE. Click the left mouse button one time.

5. A dialogue box will appear in the center of your computer screen. Read the dialogue box. It will ask you if you are sure you want to remove the file "grocery list" to the recycle bin. You have two choices: Yes or No. If you choose YES, the Grocery List file will be removed from the Grocery list folder and sent to the recycle bin. If you choose NO the grocery list will not be deleted. This dialogue box always appears when you are deleting an item to make sure that you don't erase the wrong item.

WARNING: It is very important to read these dialogue boxes so you don't erase valuable material by mistake.

6. In this example, choose YES. The grocery list will disappear from the screen. You have just successfully deleted an item from your computer.

Deleting Files and Folders: Visual Guide

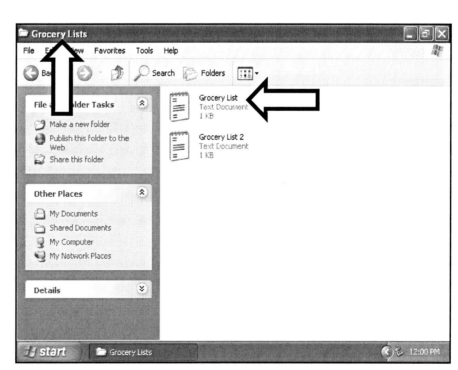

Step One: Locate the file/folder on your computer.

**Step Two:
Click one time
on the
file/folder to
highlight it.**

**Step Three:
Click on the
FILE Menu**

**Step Four:
Click the
option
DELETE.**

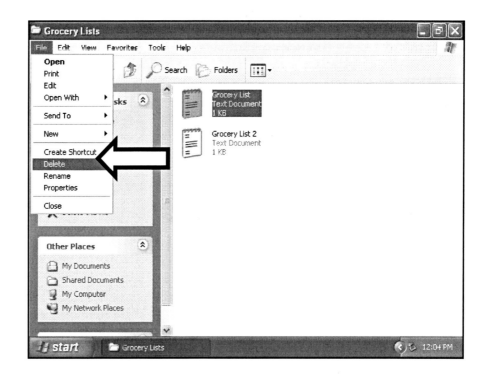

**Step Five:
Click on the
YES Button.**

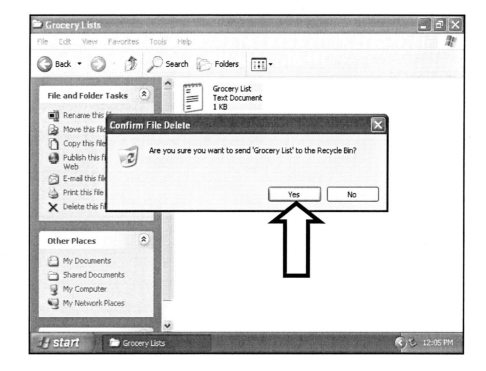

Your file/folder has been deleted.

Section 33: Removing Deleted Items from your Recycle Bin

Removing Deleted Items: Step by Step Instructions

You just deleted a grocery list from your grocery list folder, but now you realize you actually need the list. You know that, when you delete items from your computer, they go to the recycle bin. Can you retrieve something from the Recycle Bin? Yes. The first thing you need to do to get something out of the trash is to find it. The recycle bin is located on the desktop of your computer. It will be an icon (small picture) of a wastebasket. If you have any windows open you will either need to minimize those windows, using the minus sign button in the upper right hand corner of the window, or close the windows using the "X" button in the upper right hand corner of the windows. Either button will clear your desktop of any open windows.

1. Locate the recycle bin on your desktop. Place your mouse arrow on the picture of the wastebasket. Double click to open the recycle bin.

2. A successful double click will open the Recycle Bin window. It will say "Recycle Bin" in the title bar. Once the recycle bin window has been opened, any items that have been deleted from your computer will be located on the right hand side of the window. The Grocery List will be one of those items.

3. To retrieve the Grocery List from the recycle bin, click one time on the Grocery List with your left mouse button. This will highlight the grocery list.

4. Now the computer knows what item you want. Click your left mouse button one time on the FILE menu.

5. The top option in the file menu will be RESTORE. Move your mouse arrow down to RESTORE and click the left mouse button one time. Any deleted item restored from the recycle bin will return to the place it was located before it was deleted. The Grocery List will disappear from your recycle bin and reappear in the Grocery List Folder.

Removing Deleted Items from your Recycle Bin: Visual Guide

**Step One:
Double Click the
RECYCLE BIN
Icon.**

Step Two:
Locate the item
you want to
remove from
the recycle bin.

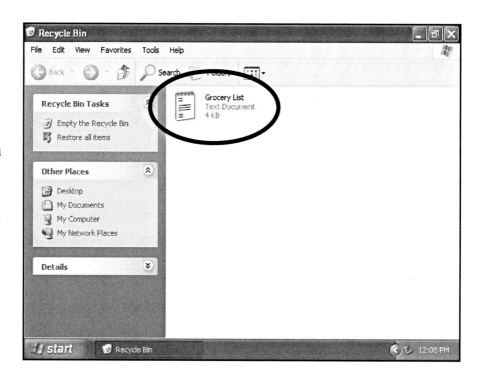

Step Three:
Click one time
on the item to
highlight it.

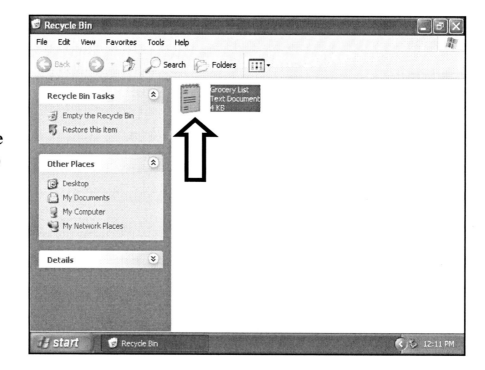

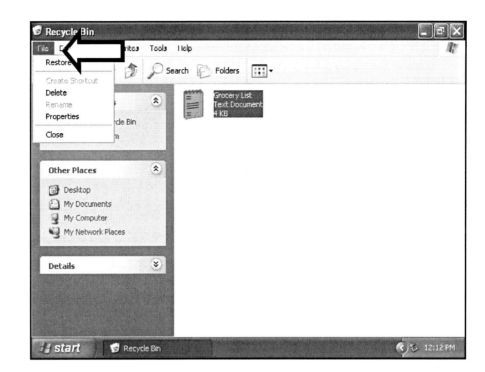

Step Four:
Click on the
FILE Menu.

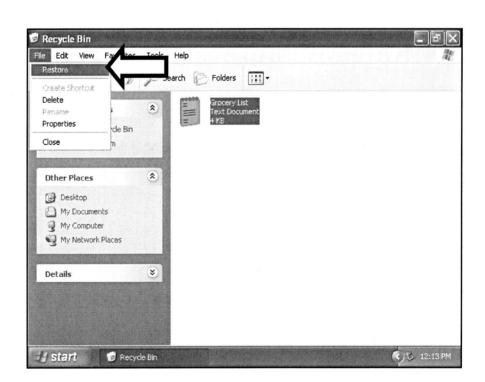

Step Five:
Click on the
option
RESTORE.

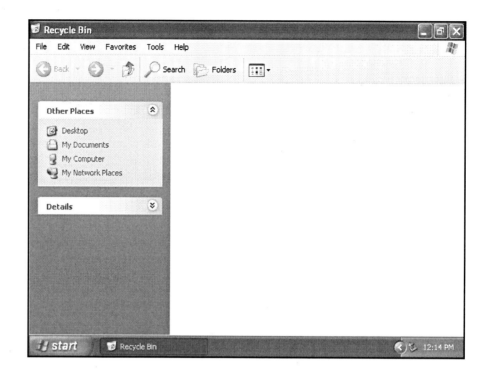

The restored item will be placed back in its original location.

Section 34: Emptying the Recycle Bin

Emptying the Recycle Bin: Step by Step Instructions

After you use your computer for a while, the recycle bin will begin to fill up with more and more deleted items. These items, even though they are in your recycle bin, still take up storage space on your computer. If the recycle bin becomes too full your computer may begin to slow down. It is a good idea to empty your recycle bin occasionally to keep your computer operating smoothly. When you empty your recycle bin, the items located inside it will be lost forever! Just like you cannot get items back once the garbage menu have taken it from the curb, you cannot retrieve any item once it has been emptied from the recycle bin.

1. To empty your recycle bin, first open your recycle bin by double clicking the recycle bin icon on the desktop.
2. Once the recycle bin window has been opened, double check the contents on the right hand side of the window to make sure that there is

210

nothing important in the bin. If you find something important, remove the item from the bin. (As described in the last section.)

3. If there is nothing important in the bin, click on the FILE menu in the upper left hand corner of the window.

4. The file menu will open. The top option will be EMPTY RECYCLE BIN. Slide your mouse arrow down over empty recycle bin and click the left mouse button one time.

5. A dialogue box will appear in the center of your computer screen. Read the dialogue box. The dialogue box will ask you if you are sure you want to delete the items in your recycle bin. You will have two options YES and NO. If you click YES, the items will be deleted forever. If you click NO, the dialogue box will disappear and the items will remain in your recycle bin.

Emptying the Recycle Bin: Visual Guide

**Step One:
Double click on
the
RECYCLE BIN
Icon.**

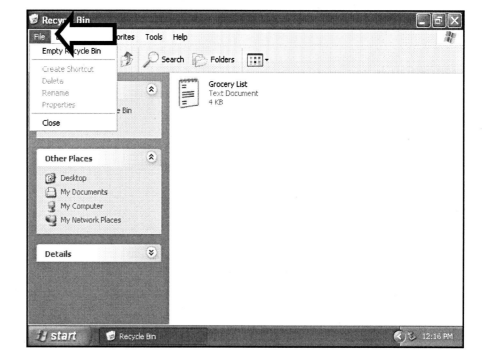

**Step Two:
Click on the
FILE Menu.**

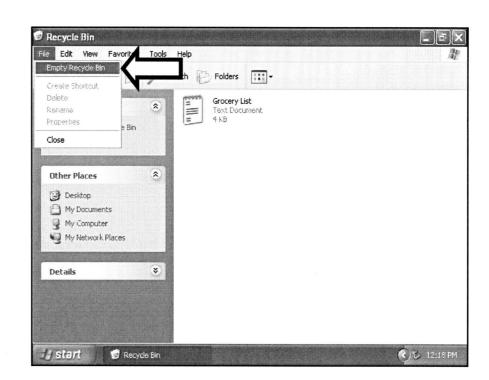

**Step Three:
Click the
option
EMPTY
RECYCLE
BIN.**

Step Three: Click the YES Button.

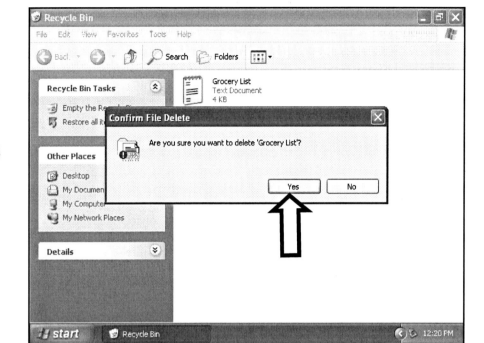

Your Recycle Bin has been emptied.

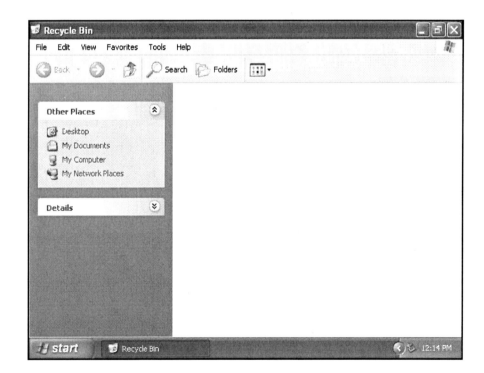

Chapter 9: The Recycle Bin & More

Section 35: Creating Shortcuts

Creating Shortcuts: Step by Step Instructions

A shortcut is a bridge between an icon on your desktop and a file or program on your computer. It enables you to gain access to files and folders without using the Start Menu. When you create a shortcut, a new icon automatically appears on your desktop. In this example, you will create a shortcut to your Grocery List folder.

1. The first step in creating a shortcut is to locate the file or folder you want to create the shortcut to. In this example, click on your START button. Slide your mouse arrow up to MY DOCUMENTS and click your left mouse button one time to open the My Documents window. Contained inside the My Documents window is your Grocery List folder.
2. In order to create a shortcut to your Grocery List folder place your mouse arrow over the folder and click the left mouse button one time. The Grocery List folder will highlight in blue.
3. While the folder is highlighted in blue, move your mouse arrow up to the FILE menu and click the left mouse button one time.
4. Slide your mouse arrow down the file menu to the option SEND TO.
5. The option SEND TO has a black arrow next to it, so a submenu will appear to the right of SEND TO. Slide your mouse arrow into the SEND TO submenu and on the option DESKTOP (CREATE SHORTCUT).
6. Click the left mouse button one time on the option DESKTOP. After you click, the file menu will disappear. You have successfully created a shortcut to the grocery list folder on your computer. You can view your shortcut by returning to the desktop.
7. Click the "X" button in the upper right hand corner of your My Documents window to close the window. Once the window has been closed, look at your desktop. There will be a brand new icon named Grocery List. The icon will have a small arrow on it denoting it is a shortcut to the Grocery List folder.

Notice that you did not move the location of your Grocery List folder. The folder is still located in My Documents. You simply added a way to access the folder without going through the Start Menu. Try it out. Double click the Grocery List shortcut on your desktop and the Grocery List folder will open on the desktop.

Creating Shortcuts: Visual Guide

Step One: Click on the START Menu.

Step Two: Click on the option MY DOCUMENTS.

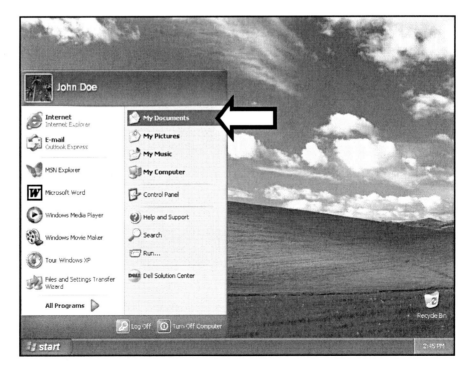

Step Three:
Click the
Grocery Folder
one time to
highlight it.

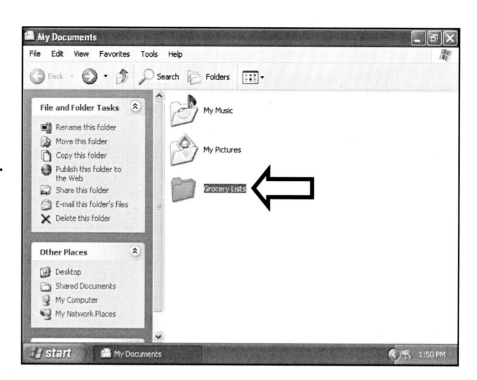

Step Four:
Click the FILE
Menu.

Step Five:
Highlight the
option
SEND TO.

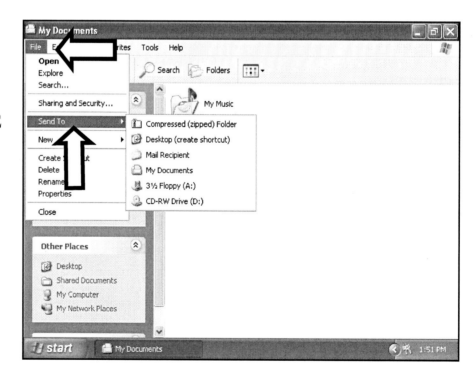

Step Six:
Slide the mouse arrow into the SEND TO Menu.

Step Seven:
Click on the option DESKTOP (CREATE SHORTCUT)

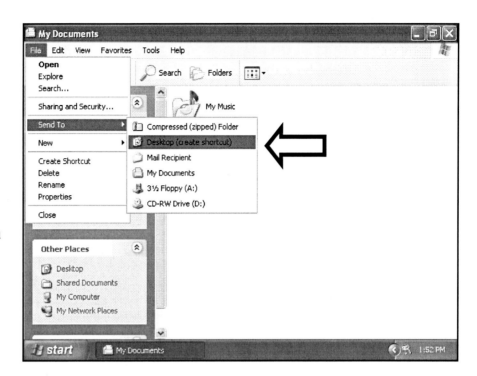

A shortcut to the Grocery List folder has just been placed on the desktop.

Double click the folder to see its contents.

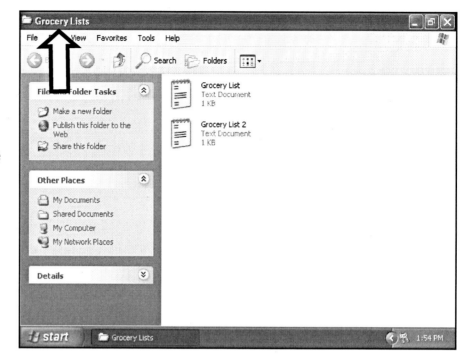

Contents of the Grocery List folder.

Section 36: Removing Icons from the Desktop

Removing Icons from your Desktop: Step by Step Instructions

After using your computer for a while your desktops may become cluttered with too many icons (shortcuts). You can remove these icons from your desktops by using the clicking and dragging skill.

1. To remove an icon from the desktop, place your mouse arrow above the icon. Press and hold down the left mouse button.
2. Move the mouse arrow over to the recycle bin while holding down the left mouse button. The icon will follow the mouse pointer.
3. When the icon is on the recycle bin, release the left mouse button. The icon will be dropped into the recycle bin.

Removing Icons from your Desktop: Visual Guide

Step One:
Click on the
icon and hold
the left mouse
button down.

Step Two:
While holding
down the left
mouse button,
move the
mouse arrow
onto the
recycle bin.

Step Three: Release the mouse button. The icon will be moved into your recycle bin.

Section 37: A Word about Highlighting

A Word About Highlighting

This book, and especially this past chapter about organizing your computer, often refers to the term highlighting. Highlighting is a very common computer term and very important to understand. Highlighting is involved in nearly every task on the computer. For this reason, take a moment to discuss highlighting and, in a way, *highlight* the term highlight.

By definition, whenever anything is highlighted on the computer screen, meaning it has a blue or black hue around it, the item is the current focus of the computer's attention. In other words, you can tell the computer what item you want to work with by highlighting it. A single click will highlight any item that *can be* highlighted.

WARNING: Whenever an item is highlighted the computer is waiting for you to tell it what to do with the highlighted item. For this reason, you have to be careful. For example, if you have an item highlighted on the computer screen and "accidentally" press the Delete key on the keyboard, guess what is going to be deleted…exactly, the highlighted item will be deleted. To avoid frustration and accidental deletions, always unhighlight any highlighted item you don't want to work with. To unhighlight an item, simply move your mouse arrow away from the highlighted item and click one time. The blue highlight will go away.

On a more positive note, highlighting is important in the steps of renaming folders, deleting folders, creating shortcuts, and many more tasks. Remember, you are in charge. You have the power to tell the computer what to focus its attention on and what not to. Below are some example highlights. Pay attention to exactly what is highlighted in each example.

Highlighting: Visual Guide

The Grocery Lists folder and its name are highlighted.

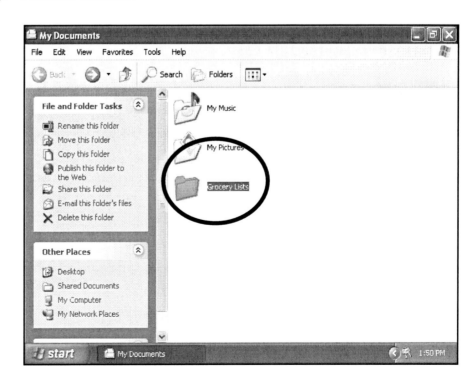

The Grocery Lists folder name is highlighted.

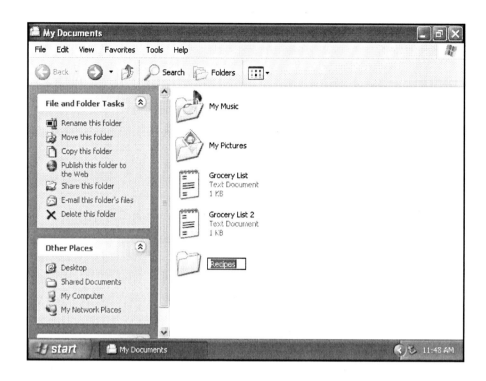

In this example nothing is highlighted.

To unhighlight an item, click anywhere in the white area.

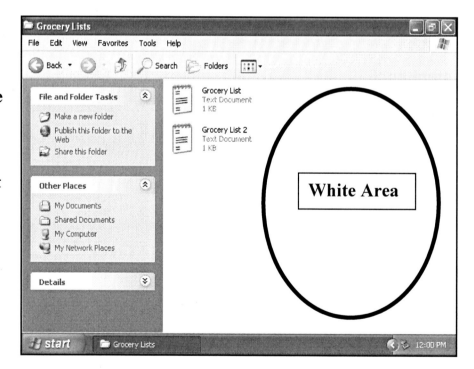

Chapter 10

Customizing Your Computer

What You Will Learn in This Chapter
- ✓ What the control panel is and where it is located.
- ✓ How to change the background on your desktop.
- ✓ How to change your computer's screen saver.
- ✓ How to make the mouse easier to double click.
- ✓ How to make the mouse easier to control.
- ✓ How to change the color schemes your computer uses.
- ✓ How to make the text on your computer screen larger and easier to see.

Chapter 10: Customizing Your Computer

Introduction
You have the ability to change how your computer looks and functions. You can change the color schemes, the backgrounds, screen savers, how the keyboard functions, how sensitive your mouse is, and much much more. In the following pages, we will discuss a few of these customizable options.

Section 38: The Control Panel

Locating the Control Panel
There is a section of your computer called the control panel. The control panel contains all the tools needed to customize nearly any part of your computer.

1. To access the control panel, you need to open your start menu. Place your mouse arrow on the START button and press the left mouse button one time. This will open your Start Menu.
2. Move your mouse arrow up the Start Menu until the arrow is on the option CONTROL PANEL. Click the left mouse button once. Your control panel window will open.

The Control Panel window will be split into two sides. The left side contains menus with different options and the right side contains different category options. The computer provides you with two different ways to view the categories on the right side of the screen. You can view the categories as icons which are called CLASSIC VIEW or you can view the categories in XP VIEW. You want to work with classic view. If your control panel does not resemble the picture on the next page, you are in XP's Category view. To follow along with the examples in this book, switch your view to classic view.

The Control Panel in Classic View.

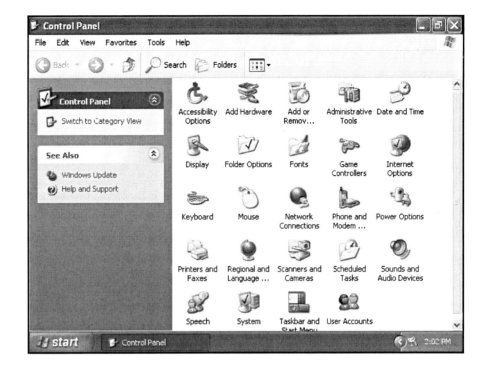

Switch to classic view by using the drop menu on the left hand side of the screen labeled CONTROL PANEL. To the right of the words "Control Panel" is a double arrow pointing down. Click once on the double arrows. The option SWITCH TO CLASSIC VIEW will appear underneath Control Panel. Click once on the option SWITCH TO CLASSIC VIEW. The view on the right side of the control panel screen will switch to the view with icons. You are now in CLASSIC VIEW and ready to get to work. You will see these directions again in the next section.

Changing Your Control Panel to Classic View: Visual Guide

Step One:
Click on the
START Menu.

Step Two:
Click on the
option
CONTROL
PANEL.

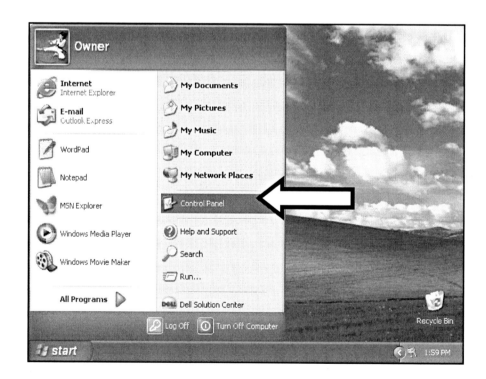

Step Three: Click on SWITCH TO CLASSIC VIEW.

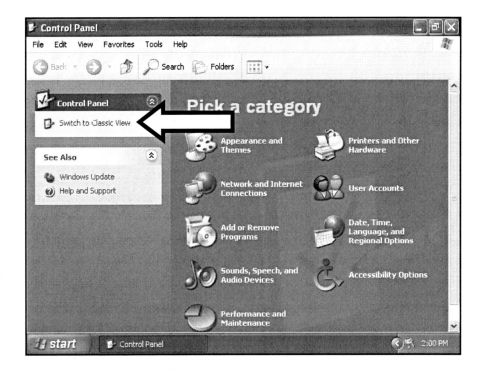

Classic View

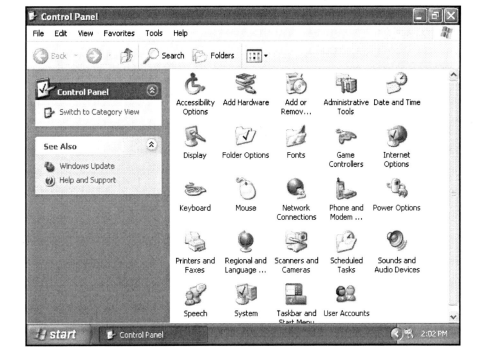

Section 39: Changing Your Background

Changing Your Background

Each of the icons (pictures) displayed in the Control Panel represent a different aspect of the computer that you can change. The Display icon is the first control panel option you want to explore. The Display icon enables you to alter your computer's appearance, wallpaper, screen saver, and other related aspects of the computer.

To access the Display icon, place your mouse arrow on the Display icon and double click the left mouse button. After successfully double clicking the Display icon, a Display Properties window will appear. This window provides you with the tools to make your changes. At the top of the window, just underneath the title bar, are five different tabs. These tabs are Themes, Desktop, Screen Saver, Appearance, and Settings. If you click on any of these tabs, you will see a different set of options. Click on DESKTOP and see what new options appear. Then click on SCREEN SAVER and APPEARANCE.

Now that you see that the different tabs control different aspects of the computer, click on the tab labeled DESKTOP. The desktop tab enables you to change the background your desktop uses. The background, which is also called wallpaper, is the picture that appears on the back of your desktop. You will see a list of different backgrounds on the left side of the display properties window. This list has a scroll bar attached to it. You can use the scroll bar to move up and down the list of backgrounds. If you want to preview a background, simply click once on a background from the list. The item will highlight in blue and it will be previewed in the preview screen at the top of the display properties window. In this example, click once on the AZUL background. It will highlight in blue and a preview of a beautiful tropical paradise will appear in the top Preview box. If you do not see Azul, use the scroll bar next to the list of background selections to move up or down through the list. Let's preview another background. Use the scroll bar to move down the list to PURPLE FLOWER. Click on PURPLE FLOWER one time. It will highlight in blue, and the preview box will change to display a beautiful purple flower. If you prefer use the scroll bar to move through the rest of the list.

Click on any that sound interesting and take a look at their previews. When you find one you like, click the APPLY button, and then click on the OK button. When you click the OK button, the display properties window will disappear and the new background will be applied to your desktop.

To view your new desktop background, minimize or close your control panel window. To minimize the control panel window, click the minus sign "-" in the upper right corner of the window. To close the control panel window, click the "X" button in the upper right hand corner of the window. After you close your control panel window you will see the change that you made to your new desktop background. Anytime you wish to change your background, simply start over with step one.

Changing Your Desktop's Background: Step by Step Instructions

1. **Click on the Start Button**
2. **Click on the Control Panel option**
   - **Make sure you are in Classic View**
3. **Double click on the DISPLAY icon**
   - **The Display window will appear**
4. **Click on the DESKTOP Tab**
5. **Choose the background you want from the list**
6. **Click on the APPLY and OK Buttons**
7. **Minimize the Control Panel window to view your desktop**

Changing Your Desktop's Background: Visual Guide

Step One:
Click on the
START Menu.

Step Two:
Click on the
option
CONTROL
PANEL.

**Step Three:
Click on
SWITCH TO
CLASSIC
VIEW.**

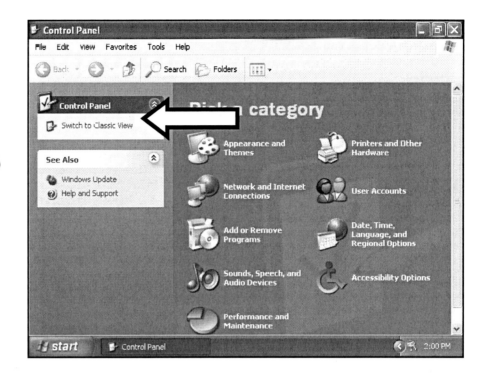

**Step Four:
Double click
the DISPLAY
option.**

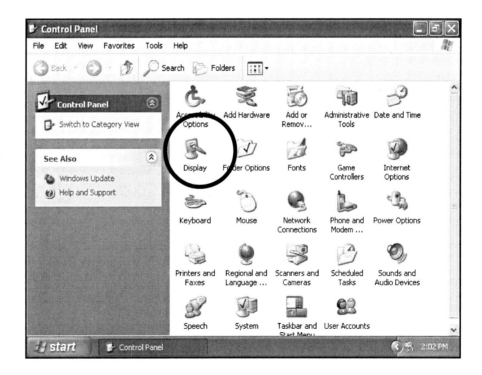

Step Five:
Click on the
DESKTOP tab.

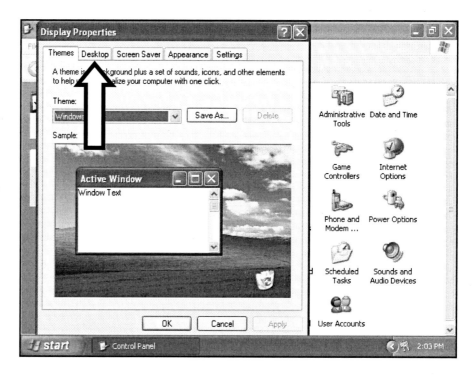

Step Six:
Click on the
Background
you want.

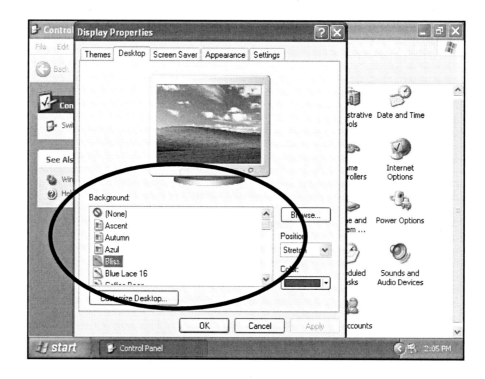

You will see the selected background picture in the preview screen.

Step Seven: Click on the APPLY and OK Buttons.

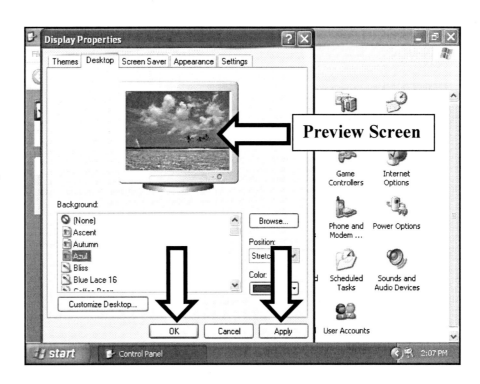

REMINDER: To view your newest desktop settings, either minimize or close any open windows.

Section 40: Setting Your Screen Saver

Screen Savers

A screen saver is a program on your computer designed to protect your monitor. It is a series of moving pictures displayed on your monitor screen. The screen saver program turns on if your computer has been idle for a set amount of time. If you've ever seen fish swimming, swirling colors, pipes building, or any type of pictures flipping through the computer screen, you have already seen a screen saver. Screen savers are designed to keep the light showing through your monitor moving, hence the moving pictures.

If you did not have a screen saver and you left your computer on for an extended period of time, the image on the computer screen would not change. Over an extended period of time that stagnant image could actually become burned into the computer screen and ruin your monitor. In order to protect your monitor, screen savers are very important.

Computers are designed with multiple screen saver programs on them. Using the control panel, you can select the screen saver you would like to use. You can also set the amount of time the computer will wait before activating the screen saver. If you leave your computer on and <u>do not use the computer</u> for a "specified" amount of time, typically 15 minutes, your screen saver will AUTOMATICALLY turn on. To turn off a screen saver, move your mouse or press any key on the keyboard.

To change your computer's screen saver you need to go to your Control Panel. Remember the control panel is located under the Start Menu. Once the control panel is open, double click on the Display Icon. After successfully double clicking the display icon, a "Display Properties" window will appear.

Chapter 10: Customizing Your Computer

Near the top of the display properties window will be five tabs. These tabs are Themes, Desktop, Screen Saver, Appearance, and Settings. Place your mouse arrow on the SCREEN SAVER tab and click one time. Your screen saver options will appear in the display properties window. You will see a drop down menu in the middle of the screen, just underneath the words "Screen Saver." Click one time on the arrow pointing down and a list of screen savers will appear. Click once on any screen saver from the list. The option will be highlighted in blue. This screen saver will be displayed in the preview box near the top of the window. If you wish to choose another screen saver, click the drop down menu again to re-open the list of screen savers and click on another choice.

After you have clicked on a screen saver you like, you need to choose the WAIT TIME. The wait time is how long the computer needs to sit untouched before the screen saver begins. It is recommended to set the wait time around 20 minutes. 20 minutes is a good time because it is long enough to know that the computer is not being used, but short enough not to hurt the computer's screen. You will see the wait time input box just below the screen saver's drop down menu. The wait time can be changed by clicking on the up and down arrows to the right of the wait time box. After you have selected a screen saver that you like and a wait time around 20 minutes, you need to click on the APPLY button and then the OK button. The Apply and OK buttons are located near the bottom of the Display properties window. Congratulations, you have successfully set your screen saver.

Changing Screen Savers: Step by Step Instructions
1. Click on the Start Button
2. Click on the Control Panel option
3. Make sure that you are in Classic View
4. Double click on the Display icon
5. The Display window will appear
6. Click on the Screen Saver Tab
7. Click on the Drop Down Arrow
8. Choose the Screen Saver you want from the drop down list
9. Click on the Apply and OK Buttons
10. Minimize the Control Panel window to view your desktop

Chapter 10: Customizing Your Computer

Changing Screen Saver: Visual Guide

**Step One:
Click on the
START Menu.**

**Step Two:
Click on the
option
CONTROL
PANEL.**

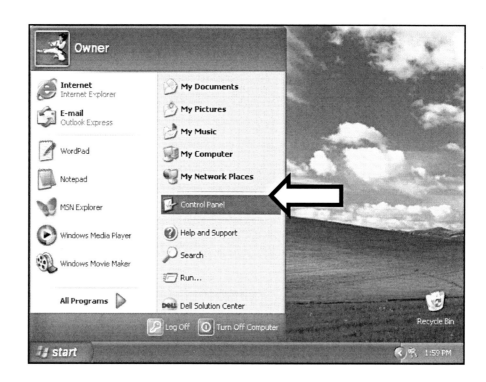

**Step Three:
Click on
SWITCH TO
CLASSIC
VIEW.**

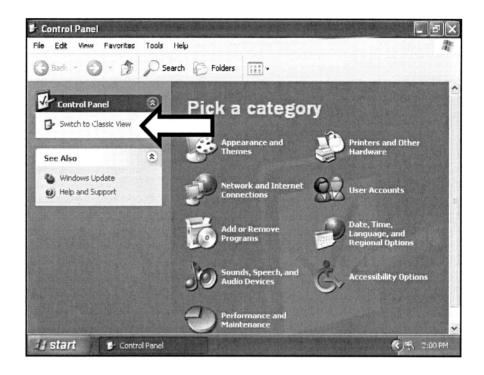

**Step Four:
Double click
the DISPLAY
option.**

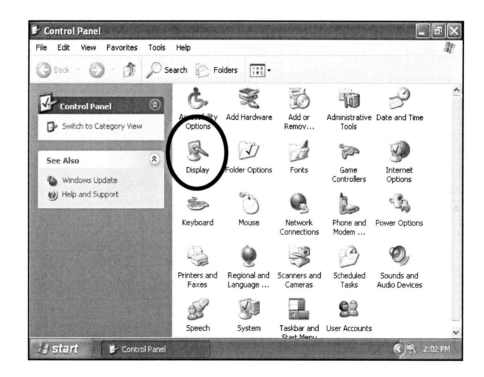

**Step Five:
Click the
SCREEN
SAVER tab.**

**Step Six:
Click the
Screen Saver
drop down
arrow.**

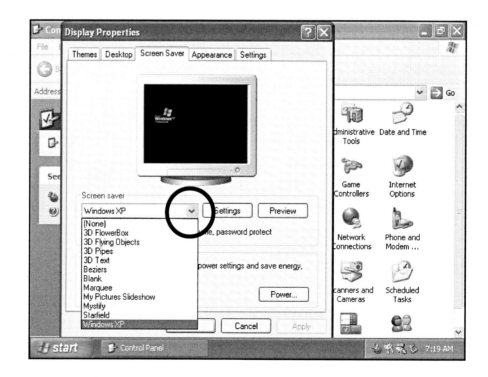

Step Seven:
Click the
screen saver
you want.

Example:
3D Pipes

Your screen
saver selection
will be shown
in the Preview
Screen.

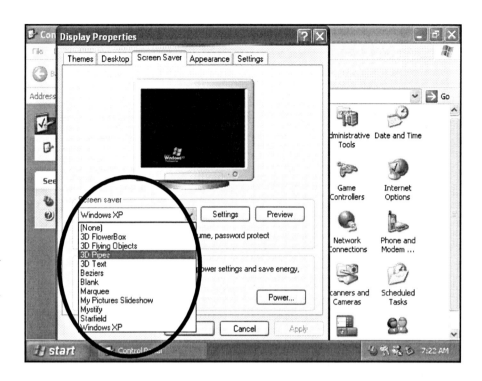

Step Eight:
Change the
wait time by
clicking on the
up & down
arrows.

Step Nine:
Click the
APPLY
Button. Click
the OK Button.

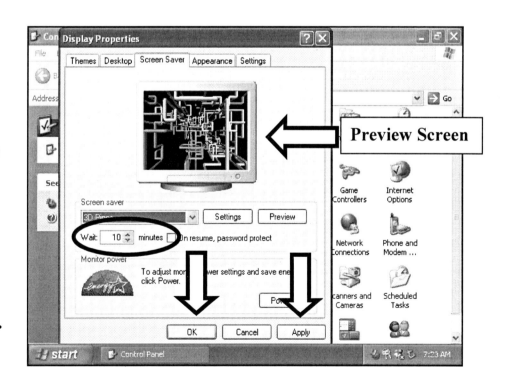

Preview Screen

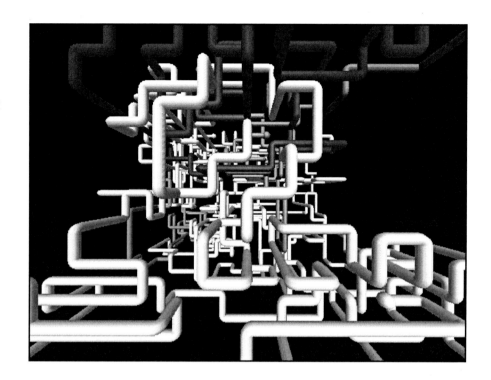

If you do not touch your computer in the specified amount of time, the screen saver will appear.

Section 41: Customizing Your Mouse

The Mouse

You can also use the control panel to change how your mouse interacts with the computer. In the following section, you will use the control panel to address two common problems. You will learn to change your mouse's double click speed. Slowing down the speed required for the computer to recognize a double click can make using the computer quite a bit easier. You will also learn how to change the speed of the mouse arrow; slow it down or speed it up to fit your needs.

Changing Double Click Speed

It is very common to have difficulty double clicking items on your computer. One of the main reasons double clicking can cause problems is that the

Chapter 10: Customizing Your Computer

computer is looking for a very fast double click. If you do not click your left mouse button fast enough, the double click will not be successful and you have to try again and again. This can be very frustrating. If you slow down the double click speed of your mouse, many of these frustrations can be avoided.

To change the needed speed of a successful double click, you need to open the control panel. Once the control panel is open, double click the mouse icon. After successfully double clicking the mouse icon the mouse properties window will appear.

There will be four tabs at the top of the window just underneath the title bar. These tabs are Buttons, Pointers, Pointer Options, and Hardware. Click once on the Buttons tab. The option in the middle of the window that appears is titled "Double-Click Speed." Just below the title, there is a slide bar. On the left side of the slide bar, there is the word "slow" and on the right side of the slide bar you will see the word "fast." In between the words "slow" and "fast" is a small gray "lever" you can move either left or right to increase or decrease the needed speed of a successful double click.

To move the lever, click and drag it. Place the mouse arrow on top of the lever. Make sure the tip of the arrow is directly on the lever and click and hold down the left mouse button. As long as you keep holding down the left mouse button, the lever will move right or left with your mouse arrow. Move the lever to the right to increase the needed speed of a successful double click. Move the lever to the left to slow down the speed needed for a successful double click. When you have dragged the marker to the desired position, let go of the left mouse button and the lever will stay in its new position.

To the right of the slide bar is a picture of a yellow folder. This yellow folder is useful to test the new double click speed. Place your mouse arrow over the folder, double click. If the folder opens up you have successfully double clicked. If the folder does not open up, try slowing down the double click speed even more. Slide the lever on the slide bar all the way to the left for the easiest double click. When you have found a double click speed that works for you, click once on the APPLY button. After clicking APPLY click once on the OK button.

Chapter 10: Customizing Your Computer

Changing Double Click Speed: Step by Step Instructions

1. Click on the Start Button
2. Click on the Control Panel option
   - Make sure you are in Classic View
3. Double click on the Mouse icon. The Mouse window will appear
4. Click on the Buttons Tab
5. Click and drag the slide bar marker left or right to change speeds
6. Test out the new double click speed on the yellow folder
7. Click on the Apply Button
8. Click on the OK Button

Changing Double Click Speed: Visual Instructions

**Step One:
Click the
START Menu.**

Step Two: Click the option CONTROL PANEL.

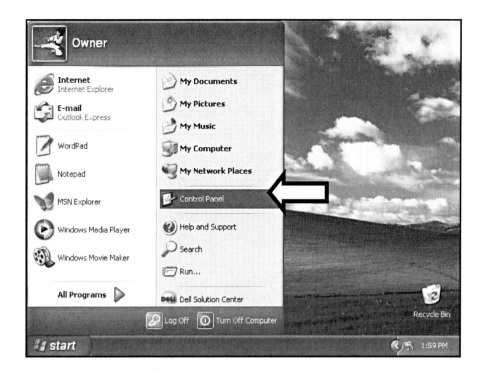

Step Three: Double click the MOUSE Icon.

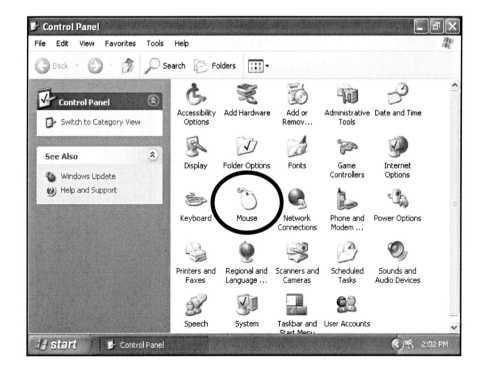

**Step Four:
Click on the
Buttons Tab.**

**Step Five:
Click and drag
the lever to the
left to slow the
double click
speed.**

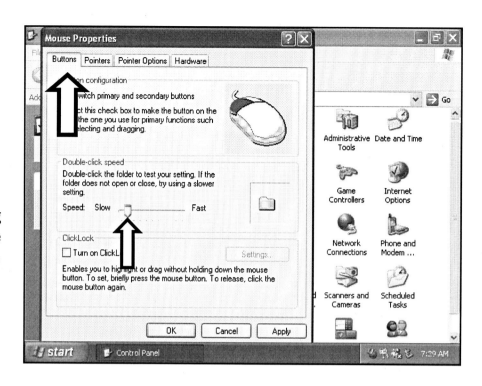

**Step Six:
Double click
the folder to
test the new
double click
speed.**

**A successful
double click
will open/close
the folder.**

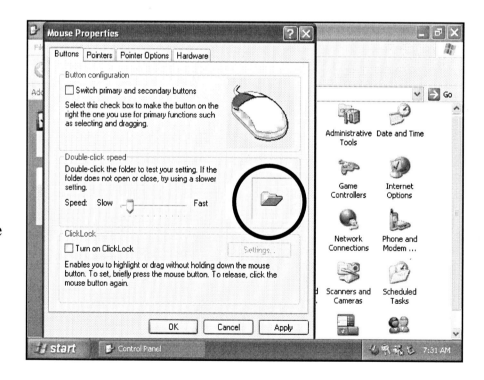

Click and drag the lever to the right to speed up the double click speed.

Double click the folder to test the new double click speed.

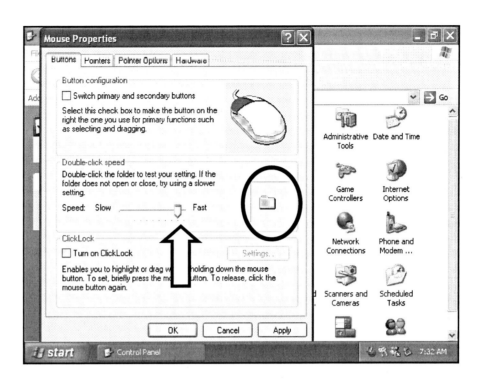

A successful double click will open/close up the folder.

Step Seven: Once a speed you like has been selected, click the APPLY and OK buttons.

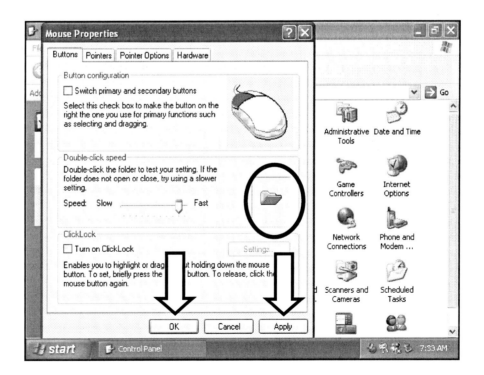

Chapter 10: Customizing Your Computer

Mouse Arrow Speed

To change the speed of your mouse arrow, you need to open the control panel again. Once the control panel has been opened up, double click on the Mouse Icon. Remember to open any icon, you need to double click. After successfully double clicking, the mouse properties window will appear. The mouse properties window will have four tabs underneath the title bar. The tabs will be Buttons, Pointers, Pointer Options, and Hardware. Click once on any of these tabs and a new set of options will appear.

Click on the POINTER OPTIONS tab once. The option that appears at the top of the screen will be titled "Motion." The Motion option enables you to change the speed of your mouse. To the right of the Motion option is a slide bar. On the left side of the slide bar is the word "slow" and on the right side of the slide bar is the word "fast". In between the words "slow" and "fast" will be a small gray lever that can be moved either left or right to increase or decrease the speed of your mouse arrow.

To move the small gray marker, click and drag the lever. Place the mouse arrow on the lever. Make sure the tip of the arrow is directly above the lever. Click and hold down the left mouse button. As long as you keep holding down the left mouse button, the lever will move right or left with your mouse arrow. Move the lever right to speed up the mouse arrow. Move the lever to the left to slow down the mouse arrow. When you have dragged the lever to the desired position, let go of the left mouse button and the marker will stay in its new position.

Move your mouse around the screen to see if you like the new speed. If you do not like the new speed, click and drag the lever to a different position on the slide bar. If you do like the speed of your mouse arrow, take your mouse arrow down to the APPLY button and click once. After clicking the Apply button, click the OK button and your new speed will be set.

Chapter 10: Customizing Your Computer

Changing the Mouse Arrow's Speed: Step by Step Instructions

1. Click on the Start Button
2. Click on the Control Panel option
   - Make sure you are in Classic View (See page 228)
3. Double click on the Mouse icon
4. The Mouse window will appear
5. Click on the Pointer Options Tab
6. Click and drag the slide bar lever left or right to change speeds
7. Test out the new mouse arrow speed by moving the mouse
8. Click on the Apply and OK Buttons

Changing the Mouse Arrow's Speed: Visual Guide

**Step One:
Click on the
START Menu.**

**Step Two:
Click the
option
CONTROL
PANEL.**

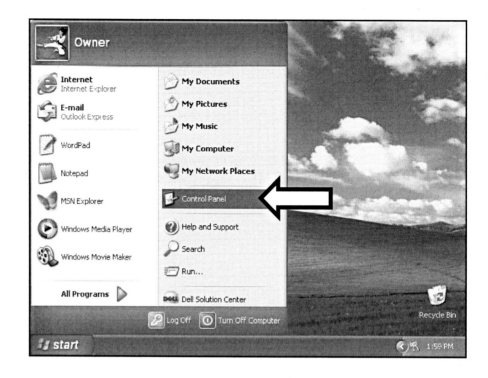

**Step Three:
Double click
the MOUSE
Icon.**

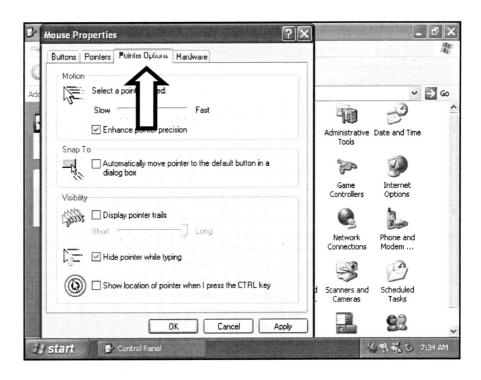

Step Four: Click the POINTER OPTIONS tab.

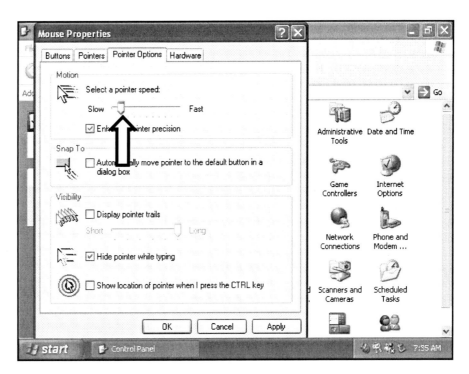

Step Five: Click and drag the lever to the left to decrease the speed of your mouse arrow.

Chapter 10: Customizing Your Computer

Step Six:
Click and drag the lever to the right to increase the speed of your mouse arrow.

Step Seven:
Once a speed you like has been selected, click the APPLY and OK buttons.

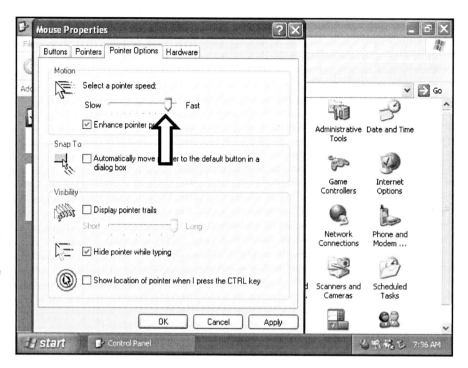

Section 42: Changing Appearance

Changing the Computer's Color Scheme

You can also customize your computer's appearance. In this section you will learn to change the color schemes and the font sizes your computer uses. The term font refers to what the text on the computer looks like such as size, style, and shape. Changing the font size and/or color schemes can often make the images on your computer screen much easier to see.

To change your computer's color scheme you need to open the control panel. Once the control panel has been opened you need to access the display icon. Place the mouse arrow on the display icon and double click the left mouse button. After successfully double clicking the display icon a Display Properties window will appear. This window provides you with the tools to make the desired changes.

Chapter 10: Customizing Your Computer

At the top of the window, just underneath the title bar, are five different tabs. These tabs are Themes, Desktop, Screen Saver, Appearance, and Settings. Click on the tab labeled APPEARANCE. Look at the appearance options displayed. There is a preview box located just below the tabs. Below the preview box are three different categories you can change. The first category is WINDOWS AND BUTTONS, the second category is COLOR SCHEME and the third category is FONT SIZE. Each of these categories is actually a drop down menu. You know these are drop down menus because of the arrow pointing down next to each options.

Click one time on the arrow pointing down to the right of COLOR SCHEME. A menu of three options will appear. The options are Default (Blue), Olive Green, and Silver. Single click on any of these options and an example of the color scheme will display in the preview box. If you do not like the new color scheme, go back to your drop down menu and choose another option. If you want to try the new color scheme, click the Apply button. After you click the APPLY button, click the OK button.

Changing your Color Scheme: Step by Step Instructions

1. **Click on the Start Button**
2. **Click on the Control Panel option**
   - **Make sure you are in Classic View**
3. **Double click on the Display icon**
4. **The Display window will appear**
5. **Click on the Appearance Tab**
6. **Click on the Color Scheme drop down arrow**
7. **Click on Default, Olive, or Silver**
8. **Click on the Apply Button**
9. **Click on the OK Button**

Changing your Color Scheme: Visual Guide

**Step One:
Click on the
START Menu.**

**Step Two:
Click the
option
CONTROL
PANEL.**

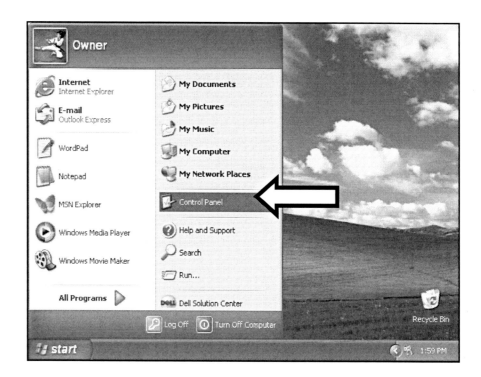

**Step Three:
Double click
the DISPLAY
Icon to open it.**

**Step Four:
Click on the
APPEARANCE
tab.**

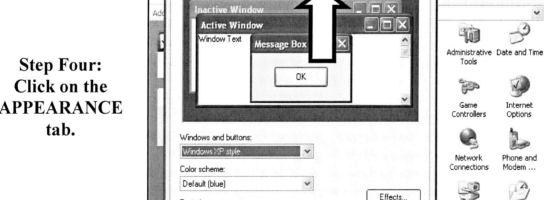

Step Five:
Click on the
drop down
arrow next to
Color Scheme.

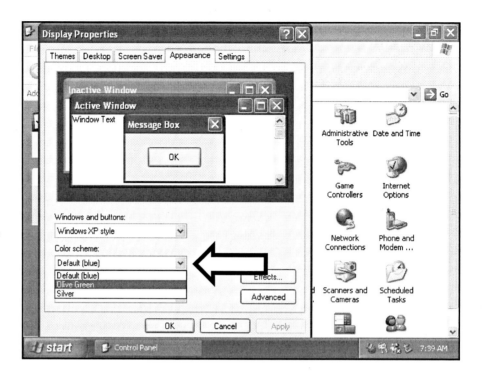

Step Six:
Click on the
option you
want.

Example:
Olive Green

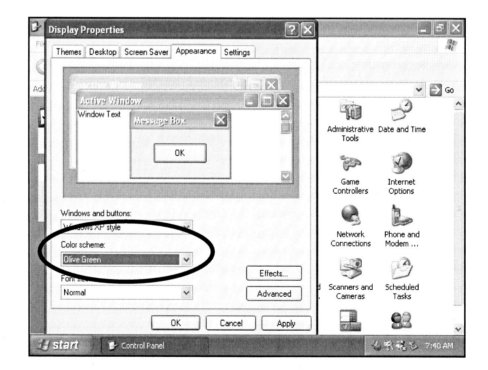

Chapter 10: Customizing Your Computer

Changing Font Size (the size of the computer's text)

To change the font sizes your computer uses, open the control panel. Next, access the display icon. Place the mouse arrow on the display icon and double click the left mouse button. After successfully double clicking the display icon, a display properties window will appear. At the top of the window, just underneath the title bar, are five different tabs. These tabs are Themes, Desktop, Screen Saver, Appearance, and Settings.

Click on the tab labeled Appearance. Take a look at the appearance options displayed. Again, as you just saw in the last section, you have a preview box just below the tabs and, below the preview box, three different categories: Windows and Buttons, Color Scheme, and Font Size. Click one time on the arrow pointing down to the right of Font size. A menu of three options will appear. The options are Normal, Large Fonts, and Extra Large Fonts. Click any of these options and the new font size will be displayed in the preview box. If you like the larger font sizes, click the Apply button. After clicking the Apply button, click on the OK button. If you don't like the changed font size, return to the Font Size category and choose Normal. Your fonts will return to their normal setting.

Changing the Font Size: Step by Step Instructions
1. **Click on the Start Button**
2. **Click on the Control Panel option**
   - **Make sure that you are in Classic View**
3. **Double click on the Display icon. The Display window will appear**
4. **Click on the Appearance Tab**
5. **Click on the Font Size drop down arrow**
6. **Click on either Normal, Large or Extra Large**
7. **Click on the Apply and OK Buttons**

Chapter 10: Customizing Your Computer

Changing Font Size: Visual Instructions

Step One:
Click the
START button.

Step Two:
Click the
option
CONTROL
PANEL.

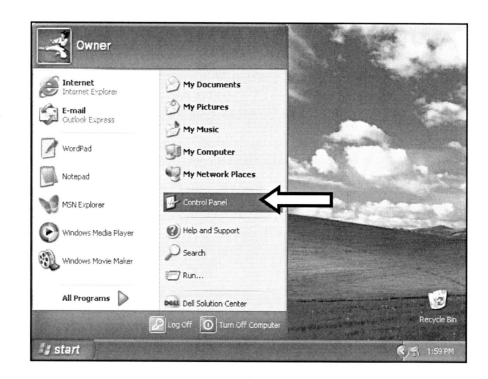

Step Three:
Double click
the DISPLAY
Icon.

Step Four:
Click the
APPEARANCE
tab.

Step Five:
Click the drop
down arrow next
to FONT SIZE.

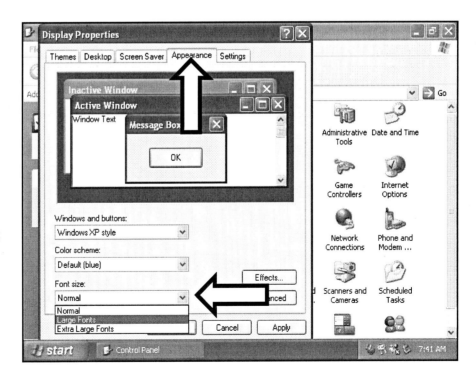

**Step Six:
Click on
NORMAL,
LARGE, or
EXTRA
LARGE.**

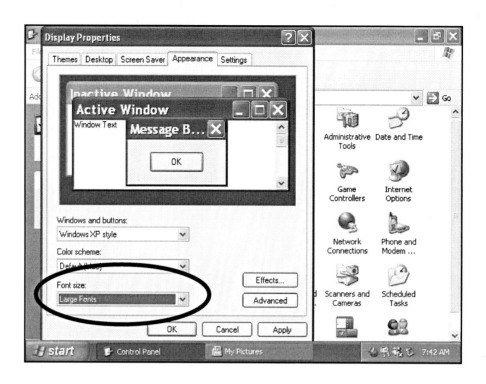

Chapter 11

Installing New Software

What You Will Learn in This Chapter
- ✓ The definition of hardware.
- ✓ The definition of software.
- ✓ How to add, install, a new program to your computer.

Chapter 11: Installing New Software

Section 43: Installation

Hardware vs. Software

Anytime you want to add something to your computer you have to go through a process called installation. Installation is the process of taking information from somewhere outside of the computer, such as a compact disk, and transferring the information to your computer. There are two basic types of installations. You can install "hardware" or you can install "software." Installing hardware means adding a piece of equipment to your computer such as a printer, fax, or scanner. Installing software means adding a program to your computer such as a game, word processing program, or instructions for your computer on how to use a new piece of equipment. Understanding the process of installing a new program to your computer is a very necessary skill. Following along in this book will help you feel comfortable about installing programs.

Most installations take place from compact disks (CD's). If you go to the store and buy a new program for your computer, you will come home with a CD containing the program. This is also true if you go to the store and purchase a new piece of equipment, such as a printer, for your computer. The printer will come with a CD. The CD will contain the information necessary for your computer and new printer to interact correctly together. In the case of the printer, you would have to install the printer's information to your computer from the CD. The following section will provide you with guidelines on installing something to your computer.

The Installation Process

The installation process may vary depending upon what you are installing, but here are some general guidelines that will definitely help you.

Your first step is to turn your computer on.

Chapter 11: Installing New Software

 WARNING: After turning your computer on make sure that NO programs are running. You do not want any games of Solitaire or any half written letters open on your computer. If you begin installing a program to your computer and you have other programs running at the same time, you may cause problems with the installation.

The second step is to insert the CD into your computer's CD ROM Drive. After you insert the CD, the computer should recognize that you inserted a CD and automatically start the installation. After you insert the CD, your job is to read and follow the directions that will appear on the computer screen. In 90% of installations all you have to do is use your mouse to click on the OK or NEXT buttons as the computer moves through the installation process. Most of the time during installations, if you don't know what a particular screen is asking, the computer will answer the question correctly for you if you simply click the OK button.

The computer will tell you when it has finished installing the new program. When it has finished, remove the CD and restart your computer, unless the computer tells you differently. Once again, the most important part of installation is remembering to read each window that appears on the computer screen during installation and following the directions.

To help illustrate the installation process you will go through the installation process of a common computer program called Adobe Acrobat Reader.

HINT: OK buttons are the same thing as NEXT buttons.

Installation Process: Step by Step Instructions
1. **Turn the computer on**
2. **Insert the CD containing the program into the CD ROM drive**
3. **The introduction screen welcomes you to the installation process and reminds you to close any other programs you may have running on the computer. If any other programs are running, you are instructed to cancel the installation process by clicking the CANCEL button. Close the programs and start over. If no other programs**

are running, click the OK button.

4. The next screen asks you where you want to install the new information. What part of the computer do you want to store your new program? The computer always answers this for us. Unless you are a super computer user, you just want to acknowledge that the computer is placing this information in one of its storage places by clicking the OK button.

5. Adobe Acrobat Reader is installed. Click the OK button.

6. When the computer has finished the installation process, remove the CD from the computer (unless directed by the computer to do otherwise.)

7. Restart your computer.

Installation Process: Visual Guide

The **INTRODUCTION** Screen tells you to close any other programs currently running on your computer.

Click the NEXT Button.

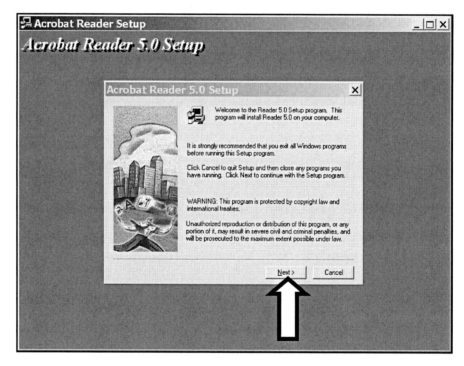

The CHOOSE
DESTINATION
LOCATION
Screen tells you
where the
program will be
stored on your
computer. Click
the NEXT
Button.

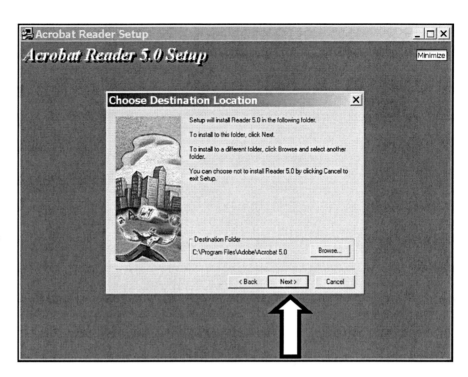

The program is
copying itself
to your
computer.

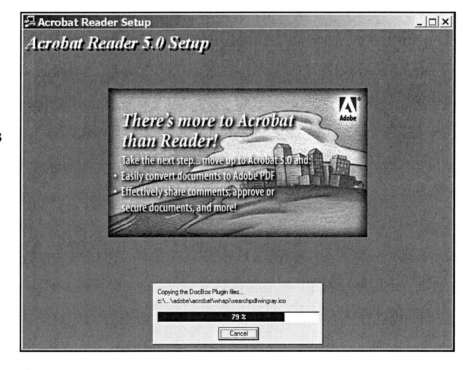

The
Installation is
complete.

Click the OK
Button.

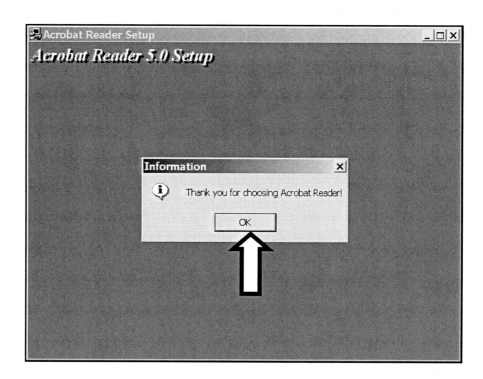

Computer & Internet Terminology
From

**Including a FREE BONUS section
on commonly used acronyms for
chat rooms & instant messenger programs.**

Appendix

@

Pronounced "at" and commonly referred to as the "at sign." Used in E-mail addresses to separate the name of the user from the user's E-mail service provider. Located above the number 2 on the keyboard. Typed by holding down the shift-key and hitting the number 2 key at the same time.

Access

v. Gain entry into a program or to retrieve information.

n. A database program created by Microsoft. It is used to store information.

Address

The specific (unique) location of a web site, file, or e-mail user found on the Internet.

Address Book

A feature of e-mail that allows the user to save names and e-mail addresses for future reference.

Applet

A small application or program that requires another program to run.

Application

A program on a computer designed to perform a specific task or function.

Authentication

A validation technique used to insure a person is actually who he or she claims to be. This is accomplished by requiring the individual to type in a username and password, which is then verified.

B

Backup

v. Copy computer files to another storage media (for example, information can be copied from your hard drive to a floppy disk). Can be used to restore lost data.

Bandwidth

The amount of data that can be transferred across communication lines, measured in bps (bits-per-second).

Banner

An image displayed on a web site for the purpose of advertising.

Bps

(Bits-per-second) A measurement of a communication line's bandwidth. Approximately thirty-two bits define one letter in the alphabet. A 56K modem can transfer 56,000 bits per second.

Blog

A journal, typically updated daily, which is available on the web. Updating a blog (journal) is called "blogging" and someone who keeps a blog is a "blogger."

Bookmark

v. Save the address of a web site to your computer for future reference. The list can be accessed by clicking on the bookmark button located at the top of your screen when you use "Netscape" to browse the Internet. Bookmarks are called Favorites in "Internet Explorer."

Boot

v. Start your computer. The act of restarting it is called rebooting.

Browser

The program used to navigate and view information on the Internet. "Internet Explorer" and ''Netscape Navigator" are the most widely used browsers.

Bug

A flaw in the design of a program resulting in the program not running correctly. Also Larry's last name (see first page.)

C

Cable Modem

Similar to a standard modem, except it uses your cable line to transfer data. It is approximately 30 times faster than a standard modem.

Cache

A memory space used to store information that is frequently accessed by your computer. It provides information at a faster pace.

Cartridge

Ink container for printer.

CD-RW

A compact disk format that allows you to repeatedly record data onto the disk. Commonly referred to as re-writeable.

Chat Room

A location on the Internet where two or more people can communicate in real time. Most frequently done through typing short messages which are then displayed to the group.

Appendix

Click

v. Press the button on the mouse. The left button is the most commonly used. The right button brings up a menu of shortcuts appropriate to the current task.

Client

Term used to describe either the computer or individual retrieving information from another source (Server). Commonly referred to as: Client - Server relationship.

Clip Art

Pictures designed specifically for insertion into documents.

Clipboard

Temporary holding space in the computer, in which you store information until you are ready to use it elsewhere.

Compact Disc

(CD) A small, round, plastic disc used to retrieve and play digital files. Commonly used for audio, video, and large data files (for example, music and programs.) Rewriteable CD's allow the user to record and store files on disc.

Compress

v. Shrink the size of a file by using a program designed for that purpose. This is commonly done to speed up the file transfer process or conserve space on a computer.

Computer Interface

A means of interacting with your computer to access data and provide instructions to your computer (for example, keyboard, mouse, scanner, etc.)

Cookie

Term referring to a small piece of information that a web site puts on your computer. The web site's computer is set to retrieve the cookie each time you visit the site. The cookie does not let the company's computer read all the information that you have stored on your computer. Cookies were designed to help make websites easier to use. For example, an e-mail provider may automatically load your password into the box after you type in your sign-in name. This is accomplished by using a cookie.

Copy and Paste

Process used to copy text from one part of a page and then paste it into another area. Until you have completed pasting, the copied information is temporarily stored in an area of your memory called your clipboard.

Counter

A program used to count and display the number of people who have visited a web site.

CPU

(Central Processing Unit) The brain of your computer. It executes the instructions you give it. The Central Processing Unit is rated by the speed at which it can execute instructions.

Crash

Term used to explain the event when your computer suddenly stops executing the commands you are giving it. The computer stops working and must be restarted.

Cursor

A symbol (flashing line) which indicates where your computer is actively waiting for data input.

Cut and Paste

Process used to remove text from one part of a page and then paste it in another area. This information is temporarily stored in an area of your memory called the clipboard.

Cyberspace

A term used to describe the Internet and all the data that is available on it. The computer's universe.

D

Database

A collection of data that is stored in one location, providing organization and ease of data access.

Default

The starting value of some option that can be set by the user of the computer (for example, screen and text sizes).

Delete

v. Permanently remove text or information.

Desktop

Initial screen that appears after your computer has been turned on.

Desktop Computer

A computer that is designed to fit on the top of a desk. A desktop computer usually comes with a CPU, monitor, mouse, keyboard, CD-Rom, modem, and floppy disk drive.

Digital Camera

A camera designed to record its photographs as computer files instead of on traditional film. Pictures taken with a digital camera can be downloaded or scanned into your computer for inclusion in your documents or e-mail.

Directory

A grouping of files or web sites that contain the same type of information.

Disk

A plastic object used for storing and transferring data.

Diskette

Also referred to as a "Floppy Disk." A removable data storage device (approximately 3.5" square) used with computers.

Drive

A device used for storing or retrieving data from a removable storage device like a diskette.

Domain Name

A unique name identifying a web site's address (for example, www.webwiseseniors.com)

DOS

(Disk Operating System) The operating system that gave birth to Windows. Controls the computer's resources and directs the hardware components to work together effectively.

Dotcom

Name used to refer to a web site that is primarily conducting business over the Internet.

Double-click

v. Press the button on the mouse twice in rapid succession.

Download

v. Transfer information from one computer to another.

DSL

(Digital Subscriber Line) Similar to the typical modem, it uses the telephone lines to transfer data from one computer to another. A DSL connection is much faster than a typical modem.

DVD

(Digital Versatile Disk) Similar to a CD, but capable of storing much larger amounts of information. A CD can store approximately 740 MB of data, while a DVD can store approximately 4.7GB.

E̲

E-commerce

(Electronic commerce) Buying or selling goods over the Internet.

Edit

v. Change.

E-mail

(Electronic Mail) A program that allows you to send and receive letters and messages through the computer. The electronic Postal System.

Emoticons

A string of characters used to represent emotions (for instance, Happy :)
Sad :(Wink ;-) or Shocked :o

Encryption

The process of scrambling information so only the person with the correct decoding key can read it.

F

FAQ

(Frequently Asked Questions) A list of questions and answers that are asked repeatedly.

Favorites

List of bookmarks. Saves the address of a web site to your computer for future reference. The list can be accessed by clicking on the favorites button located on the top of your screen when you use "Internet Explorer" to browse the Internet.

File

Information that can be stored on a computer, disk, or cd.

Fire Wall

Security program that restricts access into specified computer systems. Companies use fire walls to keep their files confidential.

Flash Drive

A very small, easy to use, and durable device which can store or transfer large amounts of information. Flash drives are small enough to be carried in a pocket or be attached to a keychain. Flash drives are also called pen drives, thumb drives, key drives, USB Drives, and an assortment of other names.

Floppy

(Also referred to as a "diskette") A removable data storage device, approximately 3.5" square, used with computers.

Folder

Method of organizing files with related contents, similar to folders in a filing cabinet.

Font

A style describing the appearance of the letters and numbers you type on the computer.

Format

The manner in which your data is organized. Also v. Erase all information from a diskette or drive.

Forward

v. Sending the exact same letter you received through e-mail to another person.

Frames

A web site whose content, displayed on the screen, has been divided into segments. Each segment controls what is located within its area.

G

GIF

(Graphic Interchange Format) A common format in which images/pictures are saved on the computer.

Gigabyte

(GB) Approximately 1,000 megabytes; common measure used to describe the storage capacity of a computer's hard drive.

Gigahertz

1,000,000,000 cycles per second. Used to measure the speed of your computer's internal clock. Your computer can execute an instruction with each cycle (rotation) of the internal clock.

Graphics

Anything displayed on the computer's monitor that is not text.

GUI

(Graphical User Interface) Pronounced gooey. The method by which the user interacts with the computer. For example, buttons, and icons.

H

Hacker

Person who gains unauthorized access to a computer system.

Hardware

The physical parts of the computer.

Help Button

Feature which opens interactive menus designed to answer questions you have about particular tasks.

History

A detailed list of web sites you have visited while using the Internet. This list can be accessed by clicking the "History" button found at the top of your screen when you are connected to the Internet.

Hits

A count of the total number of elements used to display a web site. When someone accesses a web site that contains five images, the counter will add a total of six hits -- five for the images and one for the page on which they were displayed.

Home Page

The first web page displayed when you connect to the Internet.

HTML

(Hypertext Markup Language) The computer coding language used to create pages that are displayed on the Internet

HTTP

(Hypertext Transfer Protocol) The method used to transfer HTML pages across the Internet.

Hypertext

Any text that contain links to more information; accessed by clicking the mouse on the corresponding words. These words are commonly displayed in blue and are underlined.

I

Icon

An image representing a program or file on your computer. It is most commonly activated/accessed by double clicking your mouse button while positioned on it.

Information Superhighway

Term used to describe the Internet.

Ink Jet Printer

Printer that forms characters by spraying ink onto a page.

Instant Messenger

A program for real time communication. If loaded on both computers, you will be notified whether your friend is currently connected to the Internet. If both of you are on-line, you can exchange messages instantly.

Intranet

A network of computers used within a company to communicate only internally. Similar to the Internet, but private.

Internet

A worldwide network of computers. This network gives people the ability to transfer   information and communicate through the use of computers. Commonly referred to as the "net" or the "web."

IP Number

(Internet Protocol Number) A group of numbers that represent your computer on the Internet. This is your computer's actual address (for example, 201.109.567.98).

ISP

(Internet Service Provider) A company that provides you access to the Internet.

J

Java

A computer programming language invented by Sun Microsystems.

JavaScript

A computer programming language used in web pages.

JPEG

(Joint Photographic Experts Group) A common format for an image/picture file.

K

Kilobyte

1,000 bytes; common measure used to describe the size of a file located on your computer.

L

Laptop Computer

A computer that is smaller than a briefcase and can easily be transported. Laptops are usually battery-powered and more expensive than the desktop computer because of the higher cost to design and manufacture them.

Larry T. Bug

WWS Mascot

Laser Printer

Printer that utilizes a highly defined beam of light to heat toner to form characters on paper.

LCD

(Liquid Crystal Display) A technology used to make monitors with a flat screen and shallow depth.

Login

v. Gain access to a computer system.

Logout

v. Leave a system which you accessed by using a password.

Link

Any text or picture which gives you access to more information. More information is accessed by clicking the left mouse button when your pointer is positioned on the link. Text links are commonly displayed in blue and are underlined.

M

Maximize

v. Change the window size to fit the entire area of the computer screen.

Megabyte

(MB) 1,000,000 bytes (letters or numbers).

Megahertz

1,000,000 cycles per second. Used to measure the speed of your computer's internal clock. Your computer can execute an instruction with each cycle of the internal clock.

Memory

A computer part where information is stored so that it can be retrieved and used.

Menu

A list of options provided by a computer.

Menu Bar

A screen display on the computer which contains menu options categorized under meaningful headings (for example, "File" includes file open, save, close, print, etc.)

Minimize

v. Remove an active window from your screen, but leave it open for future access. The file is not closed.

Modem

(MOdulator, DEModulator) A device that allows two computers to communicate with each other over phone lines. It is where you connect your phone line to your computer.

Monitor

The part of your computer that looks like a TV and is used to display the information and images from your computer.

Motherboard

An internal component of your computer into which all your circuitry and devices are plugged.

Mouse

A device usually attached to your computer by a cable, used to move the pointer and select items displayed on the computer screen. On a laptop computer, the mouse is commonly inset in the keyboard.

Mouse Pad

A thin cushion that grips the ball on the underside of the mouse, making it easier to move.

Mouse Pointer

The image (commonly seen as an arrow or an "I") on the computer screen which shadows the movements of your mouse.

MP3

(MPEG-1 Audio Layer-3) A format of audio file, which is compressed helping save space on your computer. Songs recorded in MP3 format can then be played on a MP3 player. A very popular brand of MP3 player is Apple's iPod.

Multimedia

Term used to describe the different types of media available on your computer, including video, audio, and graphics.

N

Netiquette

Term given to the standard etiquette (informal rules) suggested for use on the Internet.

Netscape

A browser program which helps you view the information on the Internet.

Network

A group of computers connected together for the purpose of sharing information.

Newbie

Term used to describe a person who is new to computers and the Internet.

Newsgroup

A group of people who have a discussion through the computer about a particular subject.

Notebook Computer

Also referred to as a "Laptop." A computer that is smaller than a briefcase and can easily be transported. They are usually battery powered and more expensive than the desktop computer because of the higher cost to design and manufacture them.

O

Off-line

Describes a computer that is **not** currently connected to the Internet.

On-line

Currently connected to the Internet.

Operating System

Also referred to as an "OS." The software that controls your computer's resources and directs your hardware components to work together effectively. It also is used as your computer interface, e.g. Windows.

Optical Mouse

Exactly like the traditional mouse except that instead of using the rolling ball to detect movement, it uses an optical (light) sensor.

OS

(See Operating System)

P

Palmtop

A computer that fits in the palm of your hand.

Password

A code word (selected by the computer user) used as a security measure which is required to access specific information.

Pixel

A dot. Series of dots create your computer's images.

Portal

An Internet web site designed to be a starting point and a guide to other sites and information located on the Internet.

Post

v. Put information on the Internet.

Printer

A computer hardware device that transfers print and images shown on the computer screen to paper.

Processor

(CPU or Central Processing Unit) The brain of your computer. It executes the instructions you give it. The Central Processing Unit is rated on the speed in which it can execute instructions.

Program

Computer code which tells the computer what to do.

Query

A question that is asked of a computer. Used to retrieve specific information based on established criteria.

R

RAM

(Random Access Memory) Your computer's temporary memory. Information is stored here while the computer is in use or until the data is saved to the computer's permanent memory. If the computer loses power, all information stored in this part of your computer's memory is lost. Like a human's short-term memory, information stored in the RAM can be accessed more quickly than from permanent memory.

Refresh

v. Reload or retrieve the information currently on your screen with the intent of improving its quality.

Reload

v. See Refresh.

Reply

v. Respond to a letter received through e-mail.

Reply All

v. Send a response letter to all the people that received the letter you are replying to.

Restore

Button on the computer screen used to return the window to its original size.

Resolution

Describes the number of pixels (dots) that make up your computer's screen image. The higher the number, the crisper or better the image.

Run

v. Execute a program on your computer.

S

Save

v. Permanently store information on your computer or to an external computer device.

Scandisk

Utility of the Windows operating system that checks your computer's memory for problems and corrects them.

Scan

v. Copy an image into a computer graphic format.

Scanner

Device used to replicate a tangible image into a computer graphic.

Screen Resolution

The number of pixels (dots) that make up your computer screen image. This is measured per square inch (dpi - dots per square inch).

Screen Saver

A program that runs automatically on your computer when it has been standing idle for a designated period of time. The continuous movement prevents an image from being burned into your screen.

Scroll

v. Move the screen's viewing area up or down.

Scroll Bars

Horizontal bar, found at the bottom of your screen, used to move the viewing area left or right. Vertical bar, found at the right of your screen, used to move the viewing area up or down.

Search

v. Explore the information provided on the Internet.

Search Engine

A program that acts as a card catalog of Internet web sites. This catalog system can be searched using keywords.

Server

A computer designed to provide information to other computers.

Shortcut

A method to access a program without using the traditional menu systems. Icons placed on the Desktop are common shortcuts.

Site

A space designed to provide information about a certain topic.

Software

Programs designed for your computer.

Sound Card

A computer component that processes and delivers sound.

Spam

A message sent to someone who did not request it.

Spamming

v. Sending a message to multiple people who did not request it.

Speech Recognition

A program designed to interpret speech and convert it into computer commands. Most commonly used for dictation.

Spreadsheet

File format used in financial software to manipulate numerical data.

Start Button

Button located at the bottom left hand side of the screen providing you with access to your computer's programs, files, and resources.

Streaming

Moving data between two computers at a continuous rate. The computer does not receive all the data before it starts to use it. Commonly used for audio and video transmissions.

Surfing

Looking around and using the Internet.

T

Toolbar

A row of buttons on the computer screen that direct your computer to perform various functions. For example, the row of buttons at the top of your screen that you use to navigate the Internet is a toolbar.

Toner

Graphite material used in laser printers to imprint an image on paper.

U

Upload

v. Copy information from your computer to another computer or computer devise.

URL

(Uniform Resource Locator) Unique address given to a web site or web page.

User

Any person who operates a computer.

V

Virus

A program that makes your computer operate poorly, or not at all. Viruses are commonly transmitted when downloading information from another computer.

Virus Protection Software

Program used to detect whether a virus is currently present on your computer or is in a file you are downloading. If a virus is detected, this software will try to repair the files by removing the virus. If the file cannot be repaired, it will be deleted so that it doesn't contaminate your computer data. New viruses are created continuously and virus protection software should be upgraded periodically to detect and eliminate these new viruses.

WWE

(Web Wise Enterprises) A company that specializes in teaching computer and Internet classes to seniors.

WWS

(Web Wise Seniors) A company which specializes in designing books, classroom material, videos, and a web site to meet the special needs of people 50 years of age and over.

WWW

(See World Wide Web).

Wallpaper

Term describing the picture that is displayed behind your icons on your desktop.

Web Page

A single document designed to display information on the Internet.

Web Ring

A group of web sites that are linked together, all containing information about the same topic.

Web Site

A computer program that provides access to a web page or collection of web pages. Also refers to a group of web pages associated with a single topic.

Web TV

A device that can be used to access the Internet through a telephone line. The information and images are displayed on your TV screen.

Webmaster

A person who creates or maintains a web site.

Window

The area on the screen that is used to display programs and data.

Word Processor

A program designed for creating letters, memos, and text documents.

World Wide Web

(WWW) The part of the Internet that is available to the general public. Commonly referred to as the "web" or "net."

Z

Zip Disk

A floppy disk designed to store significantly more data than a normal floppy. A Zip Disk often holds between 100 to 250 megabytes of data.

Zip Drive

A portable disk drive used to store and transfer data.

Appendix

<u>Common Acronyms Used in Chat Rooms &</u>
<u>While Using Instant Messenger</u>

ADN	Any day now
AFK	Away from keyboard
A/S/L?	Age/sex/location?
B4N	Bye for now
BBL	Be back later
BFN	Bye for now
BG	Big grin
BRB	Be right back
BTW	By the way
BWTHDIK	But what the heck
CU	See you
CUL	See you later
DIKU	Do I know you?
EOM	End of message
F	Female
F2F	Face to face
FAQ	Frequently-asked question(s)
FWIW	For what it's worth
FYI	For your information
G	Grin
GA	Go ahead
GMTA	Great minds think alike
GOL	Giggling out loud
IC	I see
ILU	I love you
ILY	I love you
JIC	Just in case
JK	Just kidding

KOTC	Kiss on the cheek
KWIM?	Know what I mean?
L8R	Later
LDR	Long-distance relationship
LOL	Laughing out loud
LTR	Long-term relationship
M	Male
MOSS	Member of the same sex
MUSM	Miss you so much
NP	No problem
OIC	Oh I see
PDA	Public display of affection
POOF	Goodbye
PU	That stinks
RSN	Real soon now
SF	Surfer-friendly
SO	Significant other
SOL	Out of luck
TAFN	That's all for now
TGIF	Thank God it's Friday
THX	Thanks
TMI	Too much information
TOPCA	Till our paths cross again
TT4N	Tata for now
TTYL	Talk to you later
TU	Thank you
UW	You're welcome
VBG	Very big grin
WTG	Way to go!
WU?	What's up?
WUF?	Where are you from?

Thank you for using the Web Wise Seniors' Basic Computer book. We hope you enjoy learning from it. Please let us know what you think of the book and how you like it.

Feel free to send your comments and feedback
to the following address:

Web Wise Seniors, Inc.
305 Woodstock Rd.
Eastlake, Ohio 44095

OR E-mail us at
Larry@WebWiseSeniors.com

Thank You!

Web Wise Seniors is Proud to Present...
Basic Computer Manuals for Beginners

These books are the absolute best instruction manuals for beginners. WWS answers all of the questions asked by real students in our classes. There is no better way to supplement what you have learned in class. Take the computer class home with you. Each manual is fully illustrated, providing step-by-step instructions in both written and picture format. Order your copy today!

BASIC COMPUTERS FOR BEGINNERS
Topics include:

- The Parts of the Computer
- How to use the Mouse
- Opening a Program using the Start Menu
- Turning the Computer On
- Saving Items
- Creating Folders
- Emptying the Recycle Bin
- Installing New Programs
- Using the Control Panel and Much More!!!!!!

BASIC WORD FOR BEGINNERS
Topics include:

- The Basics
- Short-cuts/Tricks
- Adding Pictures and Borders
- Cutting and Pasting
- Creating Columns
- Mail Merge
- Margins
- Printing
- Problem Solving and Much More!!!!!!

To Order Call Toll Free: 1-866-232-7032

Web Wise Seniors is Proud to Present...
Basic Computer Manuals for Beginners

THE INTERNET FOR BEGINNERS
Topics include:
- What can You Find on the Internet
- Selecting the Internet Service that's Right for You
- Comparing Cable, DSL and Dial-up
- Homepages and how to Change Them
- Understanding Browsers
- Using Web Addresses
- Surfing with Hyperlinks
- Search Engines
- Creating a Favorites List
- And Much More...

E-MAIL FOR BEGINNERS
Topics include:
- Selecting the E-mail Service that's Right for You
- What makes up an E-mail Address
- Avoiding Viruses & Junk Mail
- Sending E-mails
- Forwarding E-mails
- Reply vs. Reply All
- Keeping an Address Book
- Sending Attachments
- Opening Attachments
- And Much More...

To Order Call Toll Free: 1-866-232-7032

Web Wise Seniors is Proud to Present...
Basic Computer Manuals for Beginners

EXCEL FOR BEGINNERS

Excel for Beginners introduces the many uses of spreadsheets in the home and at work. Readers will learn how to create working budgets and interactive lists, while mastering the skills needed to take their abilities in Excel to the next level. Essential topics such as sequencing, sorting, formatting, freezing, and repeating will be discussed and much more!!!!!!

OUTLOOK FOR BEGINNERS

Outlook for Beginners will help you throw away all of those yellow sticky notes and organize yourself like never before. Outlook will help you keep track of your busy schedule at home and at work. Don't get lost in the hustle and bustle of life. Readers will learn how to record important contact information, schedule meetings, send e-mail, and manage to-do lists.

To Order Call Toll Free: 1-866-232-7032

Web Wise Seniors is Proud to Present...
Basic Computer Manuals for Beginners

Notes:

ACCESS FOR BEGINNERS

Access for Beginners will take the fear and complexity out of databases. Readers will learn the power of databases and the steps to build their own databases from scratch. Whether its mailing lists, personal cataloguing, or organizing business transactions, Access for Beginners is the place to start.

POWERPOINT FOR BEGINNERS

PowerPoint for Beginners covers the basic skills needed to put together a professional quality slide show. Starting from the basics, readers will learn how to control their views, add & delete slides, insert exciting animations, develop smooth slide transitions, and much more!!!

To Order Call Toll Free: 1-866-232-7032